READING HOLINESS

A Commemorative Edition of
The Christian's Manual by Timothy Merritt;

Prefaced by Essays Relevant to American
Holiness Literature, Published in
Celebration of its Bicentennial

Wallace Thornton, Jr.

Author of
Counterpoint
From Glory to Glory
Lightning From the Past
Radical Righteousness
Sons of Thunder

COPYRIGHT © 2024 BY SCHMUL PUBLISHING CO.
All rights reserved. No part of this publication may be reproduced or used in any form or by any means—graphic, electronic, or mechanical, including photocopying, recording, taping, or information storage or retrieval systems—without prior written permission of the publishers.

Churches and other noncommercial interests may reproduce portions of this book without prior written permission of the publisher, provided such quotations are not offered for sale—or other compensation in any form—whether alone or as part of another publication, and provided that the text does not exceed 500 words or five percent of the entire book, whichever is less, and does not include material quoted from another publisher. When reproducing text from this book, the following credit line must be included: "From *Reading Holiness* by Wallace Thornton, Jr. © 2024 by Schmul Publishing Co., Nicholasville, Kentucky. Used by permission."

This volume includes the full text of *The Christian's Manual* by Timothy Merritt. It is not a scanned facsimile of a used book. It has not been "updated" or edited into modern English, punctuation or grammar, but is accurate to the author's own style and usage. The text has been carefully proofread for accuracy and formatted for easier reading by today's readers. Every effort has been made to prevent disordered text.

Published by Schmul Publishing Co.
PO Box 776
Nicholasville, KY 40340

ISBN 10: 0-88019-664-5
ISBN 13: 978-0-88019-664-2

Visit us on the Internet at www.wesleyanbooks.com, or order direct from the publisher by calling 800-772-6657, or by writing to the above address.

Contents

READING HOLINESS/5

Introduction/9

1
Paper Pulpits /13

2
Getting Egypt Out of Canaan/29

3
Cotton Candy, Cream Puffs, and Concupiscence/35

4
On Reading the Holiness Classics/41

Conclusion/47

THE CHRISTIAN'S MANUAL/49

Publisher's Preface/51

Preface/53

I
The Necessity and Nature of Justification/55

II
Of Christian Perfection/61

III
Directions for Seeking Christian Perfection/77

IV
The Most Common Difficulties in the Way of Seeking Christian Perfection Considered and Removed/103

V
Evidences and Marks of Christian Perfection/127

VI
Advice to Those Who Profess Christian Perfection/137

VII
Reflections Chiefly Designed for the Use of Those Who Profess Christian Perfection/149

Extract From a Sermon on Sanctification, by the Rev. Joseph Sutcliffe/163

APPENDIX
Biographical Sketch of Timothy Merritt/173

Bibliographic Resources for Holiness Literature/175

Reading Holiness

Acknowledgements

Grateful appreciation is extended to the *Convention Herald: Official Publication of the InterChurch Holiness Convention* and to *God's Revivalist and Bible Advocate*, the official organ of God's Bible School, for kind reprint permission for the articles adapted and annotated here which were published earlier in those periodicals.

Introduction

TWO HUNDRED YEARS AGO, the world was quite different than today. Yet, two hundred years ago, the world was quite like today.

In 1824, the Middle East was in upheaval as civil war shook the Ottoman Empire. Russia and the United States signed a treaty fixing the southern border of Russia in Alaska. American politics was in turmoil, with the presidential election between Andrew Jackson and John Quincy Adams ultimately being decided by the House of Representatives in favor of Adams. Transportation advances were made with the application of asphalt paving in Paris, France. Beethoven composed his final symphony which included his "Ode to Joy." And, as the fires of the Second Great Awakening blazed, the American Sunday School Union was formed.

In 1824, the Methodist Church was thriving in the United Kingdom and the United States. Richard Watson had just begun publishing his magisterial *Theological Institutes* the year before, while the same year saw the launch of *Zion's Herald* as the first weekly Methodist newspaper in America. In 1824, Joshua Soule and Elijah Hedding were elected bishops of the Methodist Episcopal Church, and that church's rapid growth would lead it to quickly become the largest Protestant denomination in the United States.[1]

Against that backdrop, Methodist minister Timothy Merritt had a concern that the Wesleyan emphasis on Christian perfection be preserved and promulgated among his contemporaries. His idea seemed rather modest at the time, "to furnish, in a small cheap form, directions for such Christians as are convinced of the attainableness of Christian perfection, and are *desirous* to obtain it," with the observation, "Such often meet with difficulties, and need a guide." He thus proposed to develop a guide that such seekers "may always carry with them" which would consist of a compilation of relevant writings, primarily from John Wesley and John Fletcher but concluding with "Reflections designed as Helps to a Growth in Grace" that represented an "original" composition "from the pen of a female correspondent of the author's (sic)."[2]

First published in 1824, the little guide put forth by Merritt, *The Christian's Manual, A Treatise on Christian Perfection*, had an incalculable impact that reverberates to this day. It was the first of a veritable flood of Holiness literature that swept across nineteenth century America and far beyond, including writings from the prolific pen of one of the manual's readers who through its influence experienced entire sanctification on May 21, 1835 — Phoebe Palmer, who is widely regarded as the "mother of the Holiness Movement."

Several scholars have considered the publication of

---

1. The contextual details provided here were derived from Rex D. Matthews, *Timetables of History for Students of Methodism* (Nashville, TN: Abingdon Press, 2007), 70-71.

2. "Preface," written "Bristol, Rhode Island, April 8, 1824," in Timothy Merritt, *The Christian's Manual, A Treatise on Christian Perfection; with Directions for Obtaining that State*. (New York: T. Mason and G. Lane, 1840), 3-4 (original emphasis).

Merritt's manual to be the starting point of the Holiness Revival of the nineteenth century and thus of the Holiness Movement. While it would require several volumes to chronicle the various permutations of the revival thus kindled, our attempt here is to briefly acknowledge the impact of Holiness literature in the Holiness Movement, and beyond, as a gift to be celebrated and shared yet today. To this end, this small volume gathers, annotates, and in some cases expands on, essays that have been published in various contexts over the past several years, which, taken together, serve as a preface to this commemorative publication of Merritt's seminal work.

Each of these essays has relevance to some aspect of reading and literature, with particular significance for Holiness people and Holiness literature. The first, "Paper Pulpits," provides an overview of "the role of literature in the Holiness Movement," especially noting its influence on theological developments. The second, "Getting Egypt Out of Canaan" explores how the radical Holiness commitment to the faith principle proved foundational to the success of one of the oldest Holiness periodicals yet in existence, *God's Revivalist and Bible Advocate*. The third, "Cotton Candy, Cream Puffs, and Concupiscence," warns of dangers inherent in light, frivolous reading that may be chosen as an alternative to sound, edifying literature. The fourth further encourages the reading of Holiness literature, especially the "Holiness classics." Taken together, these essays underscore not only the past significance of such literature but its ongoing relevance for those who desire to "Follow peace with all men, and holiness, without which no man shall see the Lord" (Hebrews 12:14).

Chapter One
Paper Pulpits
The Role of Literature in the Holiness Movement[3]

A LOVE FOR READING was a prominent feature of the glorious birthright bequeathed to the Holiness Movement by early Methodism. Holiness people took seriously the observation of John Wesley, "It cannot be that the people should grow in grace unless they give themselves to reading. A reading people will always be a knowing people."[4] Of course, he expected such reading to center on the Bible as the ground of all truth, with Wesley himself confessing to be a man of one book— "the Book of God!"[5] However, Wesley urged his followers to read widely, reprimanding those who confined their

---

3. Annotated and adapted from the author's article originally published in the *Convention Herald: Official Publication of the InterChurch Holiness Convention* (November/December 2018) Vol. 71 Issue 6.

4. *Letters*. VIII, 247. Letter to George Holder, November 8, 1790. Cited in Betty M. Jarboe, compiler. *Wesley Quotations: Excerpts from the Writings of John Wesley and Other Family Members* (Metuchen, NJ: The Scarecrow Press, 1990), 111.

5. *Works*. (Bicentennial edition), 1, 105. Preface to *Sermons on Several Occasions* (1746). Cited in Jarboe, 9.

reading only to the Bible— "If you need no book but the Bible, you are got above St. Paul. He wanted others too."[6]

To facilitate reading among his followers, Mr. Wesley wrote and edited numerous volumes, dealing with subjects as diverse as grammar, history, and medicine, but primarily treating religious concerns. In fact, Wesley and the early Methodists employed the full range of religious literature including biblical commentary (Joseph Benson, Adam Clark, et.al.) and theological treatises (John Fletcher, Richard Watson, et.al.). Perhaps most popular though were spiritual biographies, with accounts of characters as diverse as Hester Ann Rogers, William Carvosso, and Lorenzo Dow adding their witness to the heart-felt, life-transforming power of Christian holiness attested to by *Wesley's Veterans* and in John Wesley's own *Journals*, which still holds the record as the longest running daily journal known to historians. Such testimonials sparked similar transformations among readers so that testimony begot testimony, fueling not only the earlier Methodist revival but also the later Holiness Movement, which would keep them in circulation long after the mainline Methodist denominations had largely forgotten them. Indeed, such biographical witnesses would provide a model for the first major holiness periodical, *The Guide to Christian Perfection*, begun in 1839 by Timothy Merritt.[7]

---

6. *Works*. VIII, 315. "Large Minutes" (1770). Cited in Jarboe, 111.

7. Spiritual biographies have traditionally been popular among Holiness people. Examples include the many stories and biographies written and compiled by Anna Talbot McPherson; the six-volume series compiled by Edwin and Lillian Harvey, *They Knew Their God* (Hampton, TN: Harvey Christian Publishers), the first volume of which was published in 1974; and such works as LeRoy Brown, *On Whom the Fire Fell: Testimonies of Holiness Giants* (Kansas City, MO: Beacon Hill Press of Kansas City, 1977); Olin Garrison, *Forty Witnesses Covering the Whole Range of Christian Experience* (1888; Reprint, Freeport, PA: Fountain Press, n.d.); J. Gilchrist Lawson, *Deeper Experiences of*

Merrit's vision for this magazine sprang from his desire to make more widely accessible testimonies such as those he enjoyed in a Methodist love feast. Among the initial supporters of this endeavor were sisters Sarah Lankford and Phoebe Palmer, both at the forefront of the fledgling Holiness Movement through the influence of their Tuesday Meetings for the Promotion of Holiness.[8] Their testimonies to entire sanctification were among the hundreds featured in the periodical which was renamed *The Guide to Holiness* in 1864. During the Civil War, reports by Phoebe and her husband, Dr. Walter Palmer, from their evangelistic tour of Great Britain, became regular items in the *Guide*, helping to keep circulation strong even during wartime austerities.

The Palmers eventually purchased the *Guide*, and under Phoebe's editorship it reached a peak circulation of 37,000 from 1870 to 1873. To put this in context, few secular magazines in America had a higher subscription rate at the time. Furthermore, the *Guide* was probably in the top ten of about 400 religious periodicals then published in the United States, rivaling the circulation of the leading officially-sanctioned Methodist periodical—*The New York Christian Advocate and Journal*.[9]

Famous Christians (Anderson, IN: The Warner Press, 1911); J. O. McClurkan, *Chosen Vessels: Twenty-one Biographical Sketches of Men and Women, most of whom have been used of God in Pioneering Some Great Pentecostal Movement* (1901; Reprint, Salem, OH: The Allegheny Wesleyan Methodist Connection, 1978); S. B. Shaw, *Dying Testimonies of Saved and Unsaved* (Grand Rapids, MI: Shaw Publishing Co., 1898); S. B. Shaw, *Touching Incidents and Remarkable Answers to Prayer* (Grand Rapids, MI: S. B. Shaw, 1893); Bernie Smith, editor, *Flames of Living Fire: Testimonies to the Experience of Entire Sanctification* (Kansas City, MO: Beacon Hill Press, 1950); and George Allen Turner, *Witnesses of the Way: The Interior Life of Some Famous Christians* (Kansas City, MO: Beacon Hill Press of Kansas City, 1981).

8. George Hughes, *Fragrant Memories of The Tuesday Meeting and* The Guide to Holiness, *and Their Fifty Years' Work for Jesus* (1886; Reprint, Salem, OH: Schmul Publishing Co., 1988).

9. Charles Edward White, *The Beauty of Holiness: Phoebe Palmer as Theologian, Revivalist, Feminist, and Humanitarian* (Grand Rapids, MI: Francis Asbury Press of Zondervan Publishing House, 1986), 94.

In addition to American readers, the *Guide* reached subscribers in Africa, Asia, Australia and Europe. Similar reception welcomed books penned by Phoebe Palmer. For example, in the first six months after her book *The Way of Faith* was published in French, 1,600 copies were purchased in Paris alone, demonstrating the astounding degree to which the Holiness revival of the nineteenth century was an international phenomenon.[10]

Such popular reception not only bears mute testimony to the vast sweep of the Holiness Movement, but also reflects the integral role of "paper pulpits"—books, periodicals, and pamphlets[11]—in the development and growth of the Holiness Movement well into the twentieth century. By the early 1890s, there were over forty Holiness periodicals being produced in the United States, in addition to a vast array of more permanent literature from such publishing houses as Christian Witness, Pentecostal Publishing, and Revivalist Press.[12]

While these publications were buoyed by the high tide of Holiness revivalism, they in turn played a pivotal role in shaping the movement that birthed them. Entire groups of Holiness people became identified by their loyalty to some of the leading periodicals that drew them together in seminal fellowships, with the "Gospel Trumpet people," for instance, developing into the Church of God (Anderson, Indiana) and "Revivalist people" similarly rallying around God's Bible School and other initiatives launched by Martin Wells

10. Ibid, 29. See also, Harold E. Raser, *Phoebe Palmer: Her Life and Thought*, Studies in Women and Religion Volume 22 (Lewiston, NY: The Edwin Mellen Press, 1987). In addition to French, *The Way of Holiness* was translated into German. Its sales reached about 52,000 in the United States and "up to 100,000 copies worldwide" according to Melvin Dieter, ed. *The 19th-Century Holiness Movement* Vol. 4, *Great Holiness Classics* (Kansas City, MO: Beacon Hill Press of Kansas City, 1998), 131-132.

11. On differentiating between books and pamphlets, see Lester Condit, *A Pamphlet about Pamphlets* (Chicago: The University of Chicago Press, 1939).

12. See Vinson Synan, *The Holiness-Pentecostal Tradition: Charismatic Movements in the Twentieth Century*, 2nd Edition (Grand Rapids, MI: Eerdmans, 1997), 35.

Knapp. Indeed, much like other populist religious movements of the time, it could be said of many Holiness people that "editors wielded the power" usually associated with bishops in mainline Methodism — promoting approved evangelists by publishing slates and revival reports, soliciting for worthwhile missionary work at home and abroad, and connecting likeminded folks at the grassroots level.[13] Likewise, writers were among the most celebrated of holiness advocates during the nineteenth century.

Many Holiness evangelists found that the printed page augmented their preaching circuit and gave them a much wider acquaintance among the rank-and-file than otherwise possible. Such luminaries as W. B. Godbey and A. M. Hills credited their books with taking their ministries to a new level and opening up many doors to them and the Holiness message.[14] Indeed, some authors found that the Holiness book market could at times prove quite lucrative as the masses clamored for more instruction in the way of holiness.

One of the more spectacular "success stories" among Holiness writers was that of J. A. Wood, who went against his parents' warning that he would never see his money again and spent his life's savings to publish his first book, *Perfect Love*. The resulting sales belied their concern — between 50,000 and 60,000 copies in the United States during Wood's lifetime. In his *Autobiography*, Wood reported that "every dollar that built and furnished" his "large, beautiful, comfortable and delightful home at Lincoln Park," California, "came from the sales of 'Perfect Love'"![15]

---

13. Wallace Thornton, Jr. *When the Fire Fell: Martin Wells Knapp's Vision of Pentecost and the Beginnings of God's Bible School* (Lexington, KY: Emeth Press, 2014), 36.

14. Seth C. Rees, et. al. *Pentecostal Messengers* (Cincinnati: M. W. Knapp, 1898).

15. John Allen Wood, *Auto-biography of Rev. J. A. Wood* (Chicago: The Christian Witness Co., 1904), 58-59.

This should not be taken to indicate financial motivations on the part of Wood or other Holiness authors. Wood's response to his parents' caution regarding the publication of *Perfect Love* proved typical of the self-sacrificing attitude of many Holiness writers: "I shall do it, loss or no loss. God has directed and assisted me to write it, and money is out of the question."[16] Indeed, many of the classic Holiness books were the fruit of sacrifice and suffering. Palmer's *Way of Holiness* distills the sorrow that she felt after the deaths of three children. The publication of Knapp's *Christ Crowned Within* was financed through the sale of his "household goods," and his classic *Impressions* was forged in the furnace of affliction as he grieved the death of his first wife.[17]

Samuel Logan Brengle, who by conservative estimate had over a million copies of his eight books circulated, received none of the resulting profits which instead went to the Salvation Army in which he served as an officer.[18] He produced perhaps his most influential book, *Helps to Holiness*, as a series of articles for that organization's *War Cry* magazine while convalescing from a near-fatal injury from a brick thrown by a ruffian. Seeing this as part of a providential plan, Brengle often commented that "if there had been no little brick, there would have been no little book!" With a similar attitude, his wife, Elizabeth, kept the brick and painted on it the text of Genesis 50:20 in which Joseph told his brothers, "ye thought evil against me, but God meant it unto good."[19]

Such attitude, and the writing it produced, should not be summarily dismissed as the fruit of human inspiration. Rather, Brengle himself admitted that he

---

16. Ibid, 58.
17. *When the Fire Fell*, 12-16.
18. Clarence W. Hall, *Samuel Logan Brengle: Portrait of a Prophet* (1933; Reprint, Atlanta: The Salvation Army, 1974), 227.
19. Ibid, 89-90.

would "get into an agony sometimes in trying to write a little bit of an article. I can't dash things off instantly. I sweat and labor over my subject..." However, he freely credited the Holy Spirit's work of entire sanctification with any inspiration that his writing bore—"Out of that experience and from that moment has flowed my worldwide ministry, my preachings, testimonies, articles and books."[20] Likewise, Beverly Carradine's book *Sanctification* stemmed from his own experience of entire sanctification, with the author later writing, "I remember until today how my fingers trembled and body shook as I flung on these pages the burning experience of my soul."[21] W. B. Godbey similarly asserted that "the reason" he had written books—eventually around 200 volumes—was "the simple fact that God gave them to me."[22] Martin Wells Knapp also testified, "God filled me with messages which, like pent-up fire, must find expression. I wrote because He filled me so full I could not help it."[23]

It would be hard to overestimate the influence of the resultant "revival kindlings" on the Holiness Movement, on Christianity at large, and even on the larger culture. For example, readers of Holiness devotionals such as Lettie Cowman's *Streams in the Desert* and Oswald Chamber's *My Utmost for His Highest* have included such diverse leaders as Chiang Kai-shek and President George W. Bush. Far beyond such luminaries, these best-selling devotionals have directly influenced millions of other readers as well as inspiring many preachers, teachers, and other devotional writers, from Henry Blackaby to Joni

---

20. R. David Rightmire, *Sanctified Sanity: The Life and Teaching of Samuel Logan Brengle* (Alexandria, VA: Crest Books [The Salvation Army National Publications], 2003), 62-66.
21. *Pentecostal Messengers*, 12.
22. Ibid, 20-21.
23. Ibid, 61.

Eareckson Tada, who have in turn exponentially expanded their impact.[24]

Of particular significance is the role that literature has played in shaping the Holiness Movement through both organizational developments and doctrinal formulations. Even what may seem to be the most mundane of religious literary genres, the denominational manual, has illustrated the potency inherent in "paper pulpits," with some Holiness groups in other countries actually drawing their identity from such printed guides. For instance, such a group developed in Nigeria beginning in the 1940s "under indigenous leadership ... deriving its doctrinal beliefs and name in part from a *Manual* of the International Church of the Nazarene," but only officially becoming a part of the denomination through merger in 1988.[25] The work of the Bible Missionary Church in Myanmar is another and even more recent illustration of the pivotal role played by a denominational manual as an indigenous group embraced a document formulated in the context of the American Holiness Movement.[26] While such publications would hardly be seen as aids to church growth in the United States, they have demonstrated the compelling nature of the written Holiness witness in other countries where Holiness literature is not as common.

Aside from such organic growth, perhaps the most

---

24. See Lettie Cowman and Ed Erny, *The Story Behind* Streams in the Desert (Greenwood, IN: OMS International, 1994); Lina Abujamra, et. al. *Utmost Ongoing: Reflections on the Legacy of Oswald Chambers* (Grand Rapids, MI: Discovery House, 2017); David McCasland, *Oswald Chambers: Abandoned to God: The Life Story of the Author of* My Utmost for His Highest (Grand Rapids, MI: Discovery House, 1993); Michelle Ule, *Mrs. Oswald Chambers: The Woman Behind the World's Bestselling Devotional* (Grand Rapids: Baker Books, 2017) and *Overflowing Faith: Lettie Cowman and Streams in the Desert* (N.P.: n.p., 2023).

25. *Church of the Nazarene Manual 2013-2017* (Kansas City, MO: Nazarene Publishing House, 2013), 22.

26. See Amos Chin, "Report from Myanmar," *Missionary Revivalist: Official Organ of The Bible Missionary Church* Vol. XLVIII No. 5 (October 2003), 6.

important influence of literature on the Holiness Movement regards doctrinal identity, particularly as the movement responded to various challenges throughout its formative century. Unsurprisingly, most early Holiness books and periodicals focused on the doctrine of holiness. For the classic Holiness writers, all other issues found proper perspective only when viewed in light of this doctrine, aptly termed *The Central Idea of Christianity* by Bishop Jesse T. Peck.[27] While the primary emphasis was on entire sanctification,[28] strong collateral interests included topics with an obvious bearing on Christian experience and testimony. Accordingly, much Holiness ink was devoted to such issues as tongues-speaking, assurance and security, and competing views of sanctification.[29]

W. B. Godbey, who unsheathed his prolific pen against tongues-speaking (glossolalia), has been credited by Pentecostal scholar Vinson Synan with dissuading numerous Holiness folk from joining the ranks of early Pentecostalism.[30] Throughout the twentieth century, a veritable chorus of Holiness writers joined Godbey's warning against identifying tongues-speaking as evidence of Spirit-baptism. This proved a particularly critical issue for Nazarenes, with leaders like general superintendent John A. Knight and *Herald of Holiness* editor W. T. Purkiser joining scholars like Donald S. Metz and Timo-

---

27. Jesse T. Peck, *The Central Idea of Christianity* (1858; Reprint, Salem, OH: Schmul Publishing Co., 1999).

28. For guides to the literature, see the Bibliographic Resources for Holiness Literature at the end of this volume.

29. On various views of sanctification, see Donald L. Alexander, ed. *Christian Spirituality: Five Views of Sanctification* (Downers Grove, IL: InterVarsity Press, 1988); Melvin E. Dieter, Anthony A. Hoekema, et.al. *Five Views on Sanctification* (Grand Rapids, MI: Zonderan, 1987); Marlin R. Hotle, *In Search of Sanctification* (Salem, OH: Schmul Publishing Company, 1991); and W. T. Purkiser, *Conflicting Concepts of Holiness: Some Current Issues in the Doctrine of Sanctification* (Kansas City, MO: Beacon Hill Press, 1953).

30. Synan, 146. For Godbey's approach, see his booklets *Spiritualism, Devil-worship and the Tongues* (Cincinnati, OH: God's Revivalist Press, n. d.) and *Tongue Movement, Satanic* (Zarephath, NJ: Pillar of Fire, 1918).

thy L. Smith in an attempt to buttress the denomination against the charismatic tide that followed in the wake of earlier Pentecostalism.[31] However, the Nazarenes were not alone in opposing the "tongues" phenomenon, with the Wesleyan general superintendents issuing their own warnings against the "Charismatic Movement" and "speaking in an unknown tongue" in 1975.[32] The significance of the issue of tongues-speaking for the Holiness grassroots may be reflected even better in a partial list of other writers addressing it, many of whom were pastors and evangelists: Morris Chalfant, Gary Goodell, J. A. Huffman, B. F. Neeley, C. W. Ruth, George H. Smith, Daniel Stafford, Joshua Stauffer, George I. Straub, and H. E. Will.[33] Particularly significant in reflecting the international implications of the issue are works by mis-

31. John A. Knight, *What the Bible Says About Tongues-Speaking:* (Kansas City, MO: Nazarene Publishing House, 1988); Donald S. Metz, *Speaking in Tongues: A Biblical Analysis* (Kansas City, MO: Beacon Hill Press of Kansas City, 1971); W. T. Purkiser, *Is There A Prayer Language?* (Reprinted from *Nazarene Preacher*, Sept. 1971. Kansas City, MO: Nazarene Publishing House, n.d.) and *Spiritual Gifts: Healing and Tongues: An Analysis of the Charismatic Revival* (Kansas City, MO: Nazarene Publishing House, 1965); and Timothy L. Smith, *Speaking the Truth in Love: Some Honest Questions for Pentecostals* (Kansas City, MO: Beacon Hill Press of Kansas City, 1977).

32. The General Superintendents of The Wesleyan Church, compilers. *No Uncertain Sound: An Exegetical Study of I Corinthians 12, 13, 14* (Marion, IN: Wesley Press, 1975).

33. Morris Chalfant, "Unknown Tongues—Tomfoolery or Not?" (Danville, IL: Morris Chalfant, n.d.; Gary Goodell, *Heavenly Tongues or Earthly Languages? What the Bible Says About Speaking in Tongues* (Kansas City, MO: Beacon Hill Press of Kansas City, 1989); J. A. Huffman, *The Meaning of Pentecost and The Spirit Filled Life* (Marion, IN: The Standard Press, 1940); Jasper A. Huffman, *Profile of a Modern Pentecost Movement* (Elkhart, IN: Bethel Publishing, 1968); B. F. Neeley, *The Bible Versus The Tongues Theory*, Revised Ed. (Kansas City, MO: Beacon Hill Press, 1946); C. W. Ruth, *The Gift of Tongues* (Kansas City, MO: Nazarene Publishing House, n.d.); George H. Smith, *The Unknown Tongue*, Second Edition (Fort Scott, KS: The Church Herald and Holiness Banner, 1928); Daniel Stafford, *Speaking in "Unknown Tongues" is a Misnomer*, Enlarged Second Edition (Bethany, OK: Daniel Stafford, 1976); Joshua Stauffer, *When He Is Come* (Berne, IN: Light and Hope Publications, 1948); George I. Straub, *Pentecost Plainly Portrayed* (Freeport, PA: The Fountain Press, 1951); and H. E. Will, Revised Edition of *Charismatics and the Glossolalia: A Candid Look at the "Gift-Renewal" Movement* (Salem, OH: Alleghney Publications, 1992).

sionaries such as Wesley Duewel, Brady Duren, and Dale Yocum.[34] The cumulative effect of these writings has helped ensure the preservation among Holiness groups of an emphasis on the Giver and the spiritual graces He imparts rather than on the gifts that are exalted among charismatic groups.[35]

Even more Holiness ink has been expended in an effort to oppose Calvinistic (or Reformed) theological errors that undermine the Wesleyan optimism of grace and the doctrine and experience of entire sanctification.[36] From Bishop Randolph Foster's *Objections to Calvinism as It Is* to Richard S. Taylor's *The Scandal of Pre-Forgiveness*, Holiness writers have sought to inculcate in their readers *A Right Conception of Sin* (another title by Taylor) so that they may in turn enjoy *Scriptural Freedom from Sin*.[37] (The latter title is that

---

34. Wesley L. Duewel, *The Holy Spirit and Tongues*, Rev. ed. (Winona Lake, IN: Light and Life Press, 1974); Brady Duren, *At Pentecost—What Happened?* (Mullin, TX: Brady Duren, 1982); and Dale M. Yocum, *True and False Tongues* (Salem, OH: Schmul Publishers, n.d.).

35. For example, see W. B. Godbey, *Spiritual Gifts and Graces* (Cincinnati, OH: God's Revivalist Office, 1895), a work that was reprinted in 1975 by Hobe Sound Bible College Press, Hobe Sound, FL.

36. For general holiness treatments of Calvinism, see O. Glenn McKinley, *Where Two Creeds Meet: A Biblical Evaluation of Calvinism and Arminianism* (Kansas City, MO: Beacon Hill Press of Kansas City, 1959) and Dale Yocum, *Creeds in Contrast: A Study in Calvinism and Arminianism* (Salem, OH: Schmul Publishing Company, 1986). Also, see Jerry L. Walls and Joseph R. Dongell, *Why I Am Not A Calvinist* (Downers Grove, IL: InterVarsity Press, 2004) and Don Thorsen, *Calvin Vs. Wesley: Bringing Belief in Line with Practice* (Nashville: Abingdon Press, 2013) as well the classic—John Wesley, *Calvinism Calmly Considered: Predestination, Sovereignty and Free Grace* (Reprint, Salem, OH: Schmul Publishing Co., 2001) and *Calvinism Calmly Considered: Volume II: Law & Grace, Imputed Righteousness, Perseverance and Justification* (Reprint, Salem, OH: Schmul Publishing Co., 2002).

37. Randolph S. Foster, *Objections to Calvinism as It Is* (Reprint, Salem, OH: Schmul Publishing Co., 1998); Richard S. Taylor, *The Scandal of Pre-forgiveness: What the Bible Teaches about Faith and Atonement* (Salem, OH: Schmul Publishing Co., 1993) and *A Right Conception of Sin: Its Relation to Right Thinking and Right Living*, Enlarged and Revised Edition (Salem, OH: Schmul Publishing Co., 2002); and Henry E. Brockett, *Scriptural Freedom from Sin: A Defense of the Truth of Entire Sanctification by Faith and an Examination of the Doctrine of the "Two Natures"* (Kansas City, MO: Beacon Hill Press, 1941).

of a book by Nazarene Henry E. Brockett in response to the attack on the doctrine of entire sanctification by H. A. Ironside, long-time pastor of Moody Church in Chicago, published as *Holiness: The False and the True*.[38]) The best known holiness evangelist of his day, Uncle Bud Robinson, summed up the concern colorfully in his *My Objections to a Sinning Religion*.[39]

Holiness writers especially turned their polemical guns on two aspects of "sinning religion," which they portrayed as a theological oxymoron. First, they launched an all-out assault on what was popularly termed once-saved-always-saved teaching in books and booklets like David Anderson's *Conditional Security*, D. P. Denton's *Can A Saved Person Ever Be Lost?*, Harry E. Jessops' *That Burning Question of Final Perseverance*, and Wesley H. Wakefield's *The Bible Basis of Christian Security*.[40] Second, Holiness writers were quick to point out the inad-

---

38. H. A. Ironside, *Holiness: The False and the True* (New York: Loizeaux Brothers, 1949).

39. Bud Robinson, *My Objections to a Sinning Religion* (Reprint from Bud Robinson, *Bees in Clover*, 1921. Kansas City, MO: Beacon Hill Press of Kansas City, 1967).

40. David Anderson, *Conditional Security* (Salem, OH: Schmul Publishing Co., 1985); David P. Denton, *Can A Saved Person Ever Be Lost?* (Knoxville, TN: The Evangelist of Truth, 1983); Harry E. Jessop, *That Burning Question of Final Perseverance* (Reprint, Salem, OH: Schmul Publishing Co., 1995); and Wesley H. Wakefield, *The Bible Basis of Christian Security* (Reprint, Salem, OH: Schmul Publishing Co., 1984). Others include Mark Bird, *How Can You Be Sure? Charles Stanley and John Wesley Debate Salvation and Security* (Salem, OH: Schmul Publishing Co., 2004); G. T. Bustin, *My Sheep Shall Never Perish* (Florala, AL: Bustins Books, n.d.); John R. Church, *Security in Christ or "Kept by the Indwelling Christ"* (Salem, NC: John R. Church, 1939); Harold C. Johnson, *101 Arguments Against Eternal Security* (Springfield, IL: Harold C. Johnson, printed for the author by Nazarene Publishing House, 1935); Nelson G. Mink, *That Ye Sin Not: Studies in First John* (Kansas City, MO: Beacon Hill Press of Kansas City, 1969); B. F. Neely, *Eternal Security: A Dangerous Fallacy*, Revised Edition (Kansas City, MO: Beacon Hill Press, 1955); W. T. Purkiser, *Security: The False and the True*, Revised Edition (Kansas City, MO: Beacon Hill Press of Kansas City, 1974); Henry Shilling, *The Gift of the Gods: A Study of the Historical Development of the Doctrine of Eternal Security* (Freeport, PA:

equacies of attempts to amalgamate Reformed theology with the Wesleyan emphasis on sanctification—an effort often associated with the Keswick Convention in England and related Higher Life conferences in the United States.[41] In contrast to the Wesleyan emphasis on the purification or "eradication" of the carnal mind from the Christian in the experience of entire sanctification, the Keswick movement has advocated a counteraction or "suppression" scheme for dealing with the carnal mind. Needless to say, the theological amalgam proves to be ultimately untenable, as demonstrated both in A. M. Hill's *Scriptural Holiness and Keswick Teaching Compared* and as argued from the opposite angle by Reformed scholar Andrew David Naselli.[42] However, due to its very nature as an attempt to reconcile two opposing theologies, the rather elusive position of Keswick has proven to be a particularly insidious foe to the historic Wesleyan/Holiness understanding of entire sanctification, even though it has been successfully rebutted by such towering theological

---

The Fountain Press, 1951); I. N. Toole, *Eternal Security in the Light of the Scriptures* (Westfield, IN: Union Bible Seminary, n.d.); Matt Tiemann, *Once Saved Always Saved: The Doctrine of Deadly Delusion* (Arlington, TX: Street Corner Ministries, n. d.); Robert Walker, *Eternally Secure* (Knoxville, TN: The Evangelist of Truth, n.d.); D. S. Warner, *Must We Sin? (Conversations Between Brother Light and Brother Foggy)* (Reprint, Guthrie, OK: Faith Publishing House, n.d.); and Dale M. Yocum, *The Security of Holiness* (Nicholasville, KY: Schmul Publishing Co., 2011).

41. See "Keswick" in William Kostlevy, ed. *Historical Dictionary of the Holiness Movement*, Second edition (Lanham, MD: The Scarecrow Press, 2009), 171-173; John Charles Pollock with Ian Randall, *The Keswick Story: The Authorized History of the Keswick Convention*, Updated (Fort Washington, PA: CLC, 2006); David Bundy, *Keswick: A Bibliographic Introduction to the Higher Life Movements* (Wilmore, KY: B. L. Fisher Library, Asbury Theological Seminary, 1975; Reprint, Wilmore, KY: First Fruits Press, 2012); and Charles Edwin Jones, *The Keswick Movement: A Comprehensive Guide* (Lanham, MD: The Scarecrow Press and The American Theological Library Association, 2007).

42. A. M. Hills, *Scriptural Holiness and Keswick Teaching Compared* (1910; Reprint, Salem, OH: Schmul Publishing Co., n.d.) and Andrew David Naselli, *No Quick Fix: Where Higher Life Theology Came From, What It Is, and Why It's Harmful* (Bellingham, WA: Lexham Press, 2017).

giants as Stephen S. White.[43] Indeed, a suppression view of sanctification may remain one of the most significant theological threats to the Holiness Movement today, as many popular authors and radio teachers advocate a management approach to the carnal mind, failing to reckon with the full implications of Romans 8:7.

These issues help to underscore the vital place of literature in both promulgating and preserving the truths of biblical holiness, a role that IHC cofounder H. E. Schmul fully appreciated. As editor of the *Convention Herald* and founder of Schmul Publishing Company, he endeavored to keep classic Holiness literature in circulation while encouraging the creation of new "paper pulpits" to speak timeless truths to contemporary situations. He, like Free Methodist founder B. T. Roberts, understood that "preachers and people may backslide; but the literature remains to remind them of what they once were."[44] For instance, in light of the perennial conflicts arising from attempts to relegate the experience of holiness to a life-long process of subduing the carnal mind (i.e. progressive sanctification) rather than the Wesleyan commitment to growth in grace following a distinct, complete cleansing from the carnal mind by the work of the Holy Spirit (i.e. entire sanctification), the rebuttals of Daniel Steele against

---

43. Stephen S. White, *Eradication: Defined, Explained, Authenticated*, Studies in Holiness No. 2 (Kansas City, MO: Beacon Hill Press, 1954). See also, Stephen S. White, *Five Cardinal Elements in the Doctrine of Entire Sanctification*, Studies in Holiness No. 1 (Kansas City, MO: Beacon Hill Press, 1948); W. B. Godbey, *Keswickism* (Louisville: Pentecostal Publishing Co., n. d.); H. Orton Wiley, *Christian Theology* Volume II (Kansas City, MO: Beacon Hill Press of Kansas City, 1952), 462-463; Paul M. Bassett and William M. Greathouse, *Exploring Christian Holiness, Vol. 2 The Historical Development* (Kansas City, MO: Beacon Hill Press of Kansas City, 1985), 312; Diane Leclerc, *Discovering Christian Holiness: The Heart of Wesleyan-Holiness Theology* (Kansas City, MO: Beacon Hill Press of Kansas City, 2010), 117-118; and Leroy E. Lindsey, Jr. *Radical Remedy: The Eradication of Sin and Related Terminology in Wesleyan-Holiness Thought, 1875-1925* (Ph. D. diss., Drew University, 1996).

44. Epigraph used in Howard A. Snyder, *Populist Saints: B. T. and Ellen Roberts and the First Free Methodists* (Grand Rapids, MI: Eerdmans, 2006).

the liberal Methodist scholars of his day remain remarkably relevant.[45]

Thus, the need for such printed witnesses continues unabated. While the message of the Holiness classics will never grow outdated, there remains a pressing urgency for publications addressing current challenges such as moral relativism, postmodernism, and emergent trends.[46] Each new generation needs to have a fresh encounter with the truth so that the experiential nature of holiness is not lost. Thankfully, some recent releases from Schmul Publishing Company signal encouraging developments that hearken back to our earliest literature with its emphasis on entire sanctification as lived experience. These books, *Voices from Prison Walls* and its sequels, by New Jersey state prison chaplain William Cawman,[47] share numerous testimonials demonstrating not only that entire sanctification is alive and well, but that such experience still resonates with readers today. Indeed, it is to be hoped that such "paper pulpits" may well be at the vanguard of another great revival of holiness!

---

45. For example, see Daniel Steele, *A Defense of Christian Perfection or A Criticism of Dr. James Mudge's "Growth in Holiness Toward Perfection"* (1896; Reprint, Salem, OH: Schmul Publishing Co., 1984); *Half-Hours with St. Paul and Other Bible Readings* (1894; Reprint, Salem, OH: Schmul Publishing Co., 1976); and *Mile-Stone Papers Doctrinal, Ethical, and Experimental on Christian Progress* (1878; Reprint, Salem, OH: Schmul Publishing Co., 1984). Also, see his entry on the "Wesleyan Doctrine" of "Sanctification" in James Orr, general editor, *The International Standard Bible Encyclopedia* Vol. IV (Grand Rapids, MI: Eerdmans, 1956), 2685-2686.

46. For example, books like C. Wesley King's *Truth for Earnest Seekers: The Case for Biblical Truth in an Upside-Down World* (Nicholasville, KY: Schmul Publishing Co., 2013).

47. William Cawman, *Voices from Prison Walls* (Nicholasville, KY: Schmul Publishing Co., 2015); *More Voices from Prison Walls* (Nicholasville, KY: Schmul Publishing Co., 2016); and *Yet More Voices from Prison Walls* (Nicholasville, KY: Schmul Publishing Co., 2018).

Chapter Two
Getting Egypt Out of Canaan
God's Revivalist **and Radical Faith**[48]

WHEN *THE REVIVALIST* WAS launched in the heyday of the nineteenth-century Holiness revival, it was only one among many. In fact, over forty non-denominational Holiness periodicals were in circulation by 1892.[49] Remarkably, of all these, only the *Revivalist* continues to be published. A natural question is, "What made the difference? What accounts for the endurance of the *Revivalist*?" Of course, the answer involves numerous factors, the least not being the role of the *Revivalist* for over a century as the print voice of God's Bible School.

This relationship has been symbiotic: the school has

---

48. Annotated from the author's article originally published in the *God's Revivalist and Bible Advocate* (Summer 2013) Vol. 125 No. 5.

49. See Vinson Synan, *The Holiness-Pentecostal Tradition: Charismatic Movements in the Twentieth Century*, 2nd Edition (Grand Rapids, MI: Eerdmans, 1997), 35. On several occasions, when a periodical in sympathy with *The Revivalist* was discontinued, its publishers would give their subscription list to Knapp and let him complete subscriptions with *The Revivalist*. One notable example of this took place when the *Battle Cry* ceased publication ("To Battle Cry Subscribers," *Revivalist* [Feb. 1, 1900], 16).

counted on the magazine's constituents to support it from the time of GBS's founding through such challenging times as two world wars and the Great Depression; the periodical, in turn, has relied on school staff and students for its production and on alumni for some of its most committed readers. Indeed, it is doubtful that either the institution or the periodical would have survived past the mid-twentieth century without the other.

However, the deeper secret of the *Revivalist's* longevity may be traced to a commitment espoused by its founding editor, Martin Wells Knapp. A conspicuous feature that distinguished *The Revivalist* from many other religious, and even Holiness, periodicals was the absence of secular advertisements from its pages. To be sure, it was not advertisement-free, for it welcomed "paid notices in harmony with holiness."[50] It enthusiastically promoted religious events such as camp meetings and conventions and prominently marketed Holiness literature, reflecting Knapp's conviction that the "pen and press" provided one of the most effective ways to preach the Gospel.[51] However, Knapp staunchly refused to follow the example of such Holiness papers as the *Pentecostal Herald* and the *Christian Witness* which published ads for items ranging from farm seed to hair balsam.

While Knapp hastened to note that he did not intend "to reflect on the conscientiousness of good people who accept such advertising" since they could "have more or less light on this subject," his position was backed up with the full panoply of Holiness Movement concerns.

---

50. A. M. Hills, *A Hero of Faith and Prayer; or, Life of Rev. Martin Wells Knapp* (Cincinnati, OH: Mrs. M. W. Knapp, 1902), 83.

51. Knapp asserted that the three most effective ways of preaching the Gospel are "1st. With our lives. 2nd. With our lips. 3rd. With the pen and press." He went on to extol the third method, observing that "with the pen and press we can preach to multitudes far beyond the reach of our personal presence and also for centuries after 'Our poor lisping stammering tongues lie silent in the grave" ("Pen and Press Preaching," *Revivalist* [Aug. 1890], 2).

For example, he objected to the "worldly dressed people" featured in secular ads and to the questionable quality of some goods and services advertised. He also noted that *The Revivalist* was "read largely on the Sabbath," and he was "not clear in thrusting worldly business propositions before [his] readers on that day." Furthermore, Knapp concluded that even "wholesome" secular ads would detract from the goal of promoting full salvation:

"*The Revivalist* is my pulpit," he wrote. "Its mission is to proclaim the printed gospel…hence, I feel that nothing should enter it which does not further it. My commission does not read, 'Go ye into all the world and publish patent pills, and boom bicycles, and balsam, and baking-powder,' etc., etc., etc.; but, 'Go, …proclaim the gospel,' and I have promised God and man to 'give myself wholly to the work of the ministry.'"[52]

Central to his rationale, and perhaps most unique, Knapp rejected secular advertisements due to his commitment to radical faith—reliance on God and His people to meet the needs of ministry, whether publishing or otherwise. In Knapp's view, secular ads would undermine faith, promoting "distrust" in "God by leading publishers to depend on Egypt [the world] for help instead of on the promises" of God.[53] Knapp feared that this failure to trust would then undermine his impact on readers: "If I cannot have faith in God to help meet the expenses without depending on [secular advertisements], how can I expect God to use me to inspire faith in other people?"[54]

Such faith remained one of the most pronounced features of Knapp's ministry until his death, leading his biographer, A.M. Hills, to term him "A Hero of Faith and

---

52. Hills, *Hero*, 82.
53. Knapp, "Why We Do Not Insert Worldly Advertisements," *Revivalist* (August 1897), 5.
54. Hills, *Hero*, 82.

Prayer." Indeed, this radical faith went to the core of Knapp's understanding of relationship between God and His people. Simply put, God is "Proprietor" of all that we have. This has dual implications. On the one hand, as stewards, we are responsible to God for how we discharge our duties and invest His gifts. On the other hand, as servants and sons, we are privileged to depend upon Him to supply our needs. Knapp took both responsibility and privilege to their logical ends, ever keeping before his readers the overarching fact of God's proprietorship.

This explains why the name of *The Revivalist* was expanded in January 1901 to *God's Revivalist and Bible Advocate*. At the same time, the prominent proclamation of "God Over All" prefaced the names of the editorial staff, including Knapp's. The same logic also lay behind Knapp's decision to deed the property at 1810 Young Street to God, with Knapp himself simply listed as trustee of God's Bible School. The truth is that Knapp really believed that God Himself owned the enterprises which Knapp had been instrumental in starting, including *God's Revivalist*.

Against detractors of such use of "the Divine appellation" he retorted: "It is *God's Revivalist*. It is God's Bible-school and Missionary-training Home…. I want people to know that there is one place, one paper, one school where God is honored as the chief Head, and where the work belongs absolutely to Him. It is not a Knapp work…or any other man's, but God's. We are simply God's agents that He in His providence has permitted to carry on the work for a time."[55]

Knapp was willing to stake everything on this belief, the repercussions of which still reverberate throughout the Holiness Movement as thousands of others have been challenged to launch out similarly in faith: "Should the

---

55. Ibid, 332-333.

Revivalist die because of its loyalty to these convictions, it will be a willing martyr to its faith, and can be pointed to as a warning monument of the folly of one who trusted God, with no reliance on the sale of patent pills."[56] Needless to say, his faith was rewarded, and *God's Revivalist* continues to this day.

---

56. Ibid, 83.

Chapter Three
Cotton Candy, Cream Puffs, and Concupiscence[57]

EARNEST CHRISTIANS EVERYWHERE EXPRESS concern over the apparent lack of vital piety in the contemporary American church. In no place or time has the church been so successful in garnering property, privilege, and popularity as the evangelical church in America. Evangelicals receive Grammy awards, appear on the *New York Times* bestseller list, and frequent the Oval Office. Yet, never since the Dark Ages has the church been so ineffectual and dissolute.

This impotence manifests itself in many ways, but perhaps most dramatically in the moral decadence increasingly found among professors of religion. For example, Ralph Earle, Jr. and Mark Laasar report that "a recent *Leadership Journal* survey indicated that almost one-third of all pastors struggle with Internet pornography."[58] Other

---

57. Annotated and adapted from the author's article originally published in the *God's Revivalist and Bible Advocate* (November 2005) Vol. 117 No. 8.

58. Ralph H. Earle, Jr. and Mark R. Laasar, *The Pornography Trap: Setting Pastors and Laypersons Free from Sexual Addiction* (Kansas City, MO: Beacon Hill Press of Kansas City, 2002), 5-6.

studies reflect little distance between the church and the world regarding such issues as divorce and pre-marital sex. While evangelicals confess different beliefs, they lead lives that hardly differ from those of nonbelievers, recently prompting the conclusion in a secular newsmagazine: "Their distinctive faith aside, evangelicals are acting more and more like the rest of us."[59]

While serious saints react with appropriate dismay to these evidences of encroaching worldliness in the church world at large, we need to look a bit closer to home. Here we find some of the roots of this drift already at work among us. Although many Holiness people have stood staunchly against the flood of filth purveyed by popular media over the last century, it appears that a breach in the dike of holy discernment is ever widening.

Many who once shared a commitment to living careful, godly lives have modified or forsaken altogether their erstwhile conscientious lifestyle, now regularly devouring a diet of filth that they would have once found nauseous. What led to this tragic backsliding? How can it be prevented in others?

Answers to these questions may be found, at least in part, by considering the spiritual effect of indulgences that at first glance may seem harmless and trivial. It has often been demonstrated in history and observed in scripture that apparently insignificant practices, regardless of their purported innocence, can lead to monumental problems: *"little foxes…spoil the vines."*[60]

Of particular concern is a trend that has mushroomed among Christians during the last couple of decades—that of consuming light—albeit religious—novels, self-help books, and other frothy amusements and "info-tainment." At first glance, this may seem positive, as evangelicals

---

59. Jeffery L. Sheller, "Nearer my God to Thee," *U. S. News and World Report* 136, no. 15 (May 3, 2004): 59.
60. Song of Solomon 2:15

now have their own alternatives to Steven King, John Grisham, and Harlequin romances. However, there are several troubling elements to this development.

For one, there is the issue of **substitution**. The consumption of "fluff" takes away time for substantial reading and other activities that promote devotion and theological reflection. Even at its best, the chaff foisted by today's religious publishers on an unsuspecting, entertainment oriented Christian public (in addition to threatening Bible reading itself) stifles interaction with the writings of Milton, Bunyan, and contemporary writers who produce literature worthy of the name.

Rest assured that this is not a diatribe against reading for entertainment altogether, but an appeal for discernment in choosing spiritually helpful works and for balance in one's reading habits. An occasional "light" read may help rest the mind, but a steady flow of such reading may paralyze the mind and starve the soul. Although everyone needs "intervals of diversion from business," as John Wesley expressed it,[61] this is to provide a brief respite for rejuvenation—not permanent preoccupation with fleeting pleasures. As with eating, so with reading—while infrequent desserts add zest to life, making sweets the staple of your diet will rob you of vital nutrients and ultimately prove fatal.

In other words, the substitution of the shallow for the significant contributes to a deeper danger inherent in imbibing frothy religious entertainment—that of becoming immersed in **superficiality**. Not only are superior writings and activities slighted, but deep spirituality itself may be hindered. The focus is not on divine activity or spiritual growth but on temporal excitement and fulfillment. A search for deeper truths illustrated by the plot

---

61. John Wesley, "The More Excellent Way" in *The Works of John Wesley* 3rd ed. Vol. 7 *Sermons* (1872; reprint, Peabody, MA: Hendrickson Publishers, 1986), 33.

or reflected in character development results in frustration. The spiritual point becomes clear to perceptive readers—there is no point! It is like Wes Tracy's description of many contemporary Christians: "'Way down deep' they are 'all surface.'"[62] Moreover, excessive absorption of such material is bound to produce the same kind of people.

As if this harm were not enough, some of the frivolous religious fiction and other literary chaff so popular today goes even further in the **subversion** of the cause and spirit of biblical Christianity. Many of these works apparently take their cues from secular fiction, then project a religious veneer over the surface. In this thinly veiled guise, they actually promote unscriptural ideals and behavior. For instance, supposedly devout characters foster attitudes and engage in activities contrary to the Bible, such as dating or even marrying unbelievers. Other books exploit and distort biblical concepts, prostituting such glorious realities as spiritual warfare and end-time prophecy with sensational story lines that go so far as to glamorize violence and sensuality.[63]

Ultimately, this spate of religious fluff and foam may have another insidious impact on those who ingest it. It can serve as a subtle avenue of **seduction** away from godliness, luring its consumers to desire outright the fodder of the world. After repeated exposure to worldly enticements under religious pretext, some readers will eventually succumb to temptation and finally embrace openly sinful literature and entertainment. For they have whetted their appetite for a diet of filth by feeding on a preparatory diet of froth.

While some may stop short of this tragic outcome, how

---

62. Wesley D. Tracy, "Bedtime Parable," *Herald of Holiness* 86 no. 7 (July 1997): 9.

63. For a recent scholarly appraisal of the impact of religious fiction, see Daniel Silliman, *Reading Evangelicals: How Christian Fiction Shaped a Culture and a Faith* (Grand Rapids: Eerdmans, 2021).

many have already allowed religious chaff to substitute for substantial soul food, short circuit their spiritual growth, and even subvert their allegiance to Christ? How many Holiness people who would never think of bringing a television into their homes have found a subtle substitute in light religious reading? How many have moved from this reading to such corrupt communication as the moral sewage flooding the "information super-highway"?

Our bookshelves reflect our predicament. Even within Holiness parsonages, religious romance and adventure stories have crowded out the Holiness classics by J.B. Chapman, A.M. Hills, and G.A. McLaughlin. If the maxim is even partially correct that "you are what you read," one cannot help but wonder what the Holiness Movement will be in the not-too-distant future.

Those who would dismiss these concerns as the anxieties of an alarmist should bear in mind that, while not as immediate, the final consequence of a constant diet of cotton candy and cream puffs proves to be just as deadly as one of arsenic and cyanide. May our readers avoid the fate resulting, not just from feeding on filth, but from feasting on foam and froth.

Chapter Four
On Reading the Holiness Classics[64]

BY READING CLASSIC HOLINESS literature, you may do much toward avoiding a pitfall into which many of our contemporaries have fallen—the trap of literary provincialism. This danger involves limiting one's reading to a narrow selection of works, so that a distorted or constricted view of a particular subject, or even life in general, develops. While this practice may assume many forms, one of the most common is that of reading only currently popular works, usually written within the last few years or months.

Such a concern may seem ironic in light of this postmodern era, with its stress on diversity and pluralism. Yet, despite all the talk of tolerance and inclusion, an unprecedented exclusivity seems to grip the reading public. Indeed, this habit proves so subtle a snare that many, having fallen prey to it, actually tout it as a virtue,

---

64. Annotated and adapted by the author from his foreword for *Sparks from Seven Hammers: Reflections on the Christian Life by Seven Classic Writers* (Salem, OH: Schmul Publishing Co., 2004).

seeing themselves as up-to-date and informed when they are actually ensnared by spiritual and intellectual myopia. This frightening development has instilled an unhealthy narrowness of intellectual activity within the minds of contemporary society, including Christians, so that sermons are preached, institutions are administered, and lives are lived with little or no historical (or even biblical) perspective.

For readers within conservative Wesleyan/Holiness ranks, the problem takes on an added dimension when considering the scarcity of current publications from within the tradition. Increasingly, we turn to non-Wesleyan writers for guidance in philosophical inquiry, ministerial methodology, biblical scholarship, and even theological formulation.

To be sure, benefit may be derived from reading Henry Blackaby, Bruce Wilkinson, and other contemporary writers committed to non-Wesleyan theological traditions. Holiness people have long read with great profit such non-Wesleyan writers as Charles Finney, Andrew Murray, and A. B. Simpson. In many quarters, however, the message of scriptural holiness is in danger of being eclipsed by a muted or even mutilated presentation of the experience and relationships entailed in the life of the entirely sanctified. That is, even the Holiness Movement's understanding of holiness itself is being increasingly defined by non-Holiness writers.

When a movement's core doctrine, and thus its self-understanding, finds definition in the books and articles of outsiders and opponents, the erosion of its foundation inevitably follows. Rather than suffering "death with decorum" the movement may simply become so diluted that it simply dissipates and becomes just another element in the generic evangelical amalgam. To quote W. B. Godbey, "You must read Holiness literature, otherwise you will become weak and feeble, like carnal people."[65]

Contemporary writings from within the conservative Wesleyan tradition are thus needed desperately. However, even if a plethora of such writings is produced *post haste*—an unlikely prospect—this is hardly the time to abandon the writings of earlier generations. Indeed, to remain true to Scripture and tradition, contemporary Wesleyan writers must be grounded in the spiritual and theological works of the past. This should encompass the church fathers, the reformers, and the great revivalists, especially the Wesleys. However, it must also include the Holiness classics by such authors as Samuel Logan Brengle, Oswald Chambers, and Lettie Cowman.

Meanwhile, all Holiness people should remain conversant with classic Holiness writings. While contemporary books may help us to keep abreast of the times, only by drinking deeply at the fountains of such authors as Catherine Booth, Beverly Carradine, and Daniel Steele will we remain faithful to the legacy bequeathed us. In addition, reading their works will help to broaden perspectives and banish prejudices concerning traditional Holiness doctrine and practice—perceptions perpetuated both by hostile adversaries and well-intentioned advocates who have neglected to read the primary sources documenting the rise of the Holiness Movement. Such reading may even suggest correctives to deficiencies currently plaguing Holiness people and their churches and other organizations.

The benefits of familiarity with the Holiness classics were aptly described by H. E. Schmul in his justification for his Holiness reprint ministry:

> We obtain certain spiritual benefits by reading and

---

65. W. B. Godbey, "Satan's Sidetracks for Holiness People," in *Sparks from Seven Hammers*, 108.

studying the events, developments, writings and personalities of the holiness heroes of another day. We should study their portraits, "warts" and all.

[Today's] holiness people need to be reminded of their glorious past, and not lose sight of God's standard of piety and purity for today. Movements move away from their pristine glory into the murky fogs of ecclesiasticism, liberalism, or legalism.[66] The drift is so gradual, few are aware of the tragedy. The holiness movement today is no exception. Wesley's fear was not that the people called Methodist would cease to exist, but that they would continue as a dead appendage in the world of religions…

But what of the glory of the modern holiness people? Does it not need to recover the glory and power of a "better day"? [Holiness classics] might open our eyes, sharpen our appetites and stimulate us to a renewed effort after the "old time power."[67]

Indeed, the bold proclamation of the Holiness message by the giants of old should inspire us to new conquests. This is no time to capitulate to bland, nominal religion. Rather, this is a time to advance, and one way to do so is

---

66. These three terms were common currency during the formation in the mid-twentieth century of what today is called the Conservative Holiness Movement. "Ecclesiasticism" refers to putting human organization such as church denomination in the place of God or substituting institutional loyalty for devotion to God. For an example of concern over this threat to Holiness spirituality, see Wallace Thornton, Jr. "Reckoning with Babylon: G. T. Bustin and Radical Holiness Interaction with Roman Catholicism," in William Kostlevy and Wallace Thornton, Jr., eds. *The Radical Holiness Movement in the Christian Tradition: A Festschrift for Larry D. Smith* (Lexington, KY: Emeth Press, 2016), 149-165. "Liberalism" was commonly employed to describe spiritual or moral compromise involving rejecting or downplaying traditional Holiness standards of behavior. "Legalism" was often a charge against radicals or conservatives who insisted on maintaining such standards, implying that their hope for salvation had been placed in works rather than grace. For more historical context, see Wallace Thornton, Jr. *Radical Righteousness: Personal Ethics and the Development of the Holiness Movement* (Salem, OH: Schmul Publishing Co., 1998).

67. From an early catalog of Schmul Publishing Company.

by reading and promoting the Holiness classics, thus heeding Dr. Godbey's reminder, "You are living for eternity, and have no time to waste on transitory trash."[68]

---

68. Godbey, "Sidetracks," 108.

Conclusion

THIS BICENTENNIAL YEAR OF American Holiness literature provides a wonderful occasion to not only celebrate the glorious heritage of the Holiness Movement, but also to engage anew with the powerful spiritual writings that it has produced. Your life will undoubtedly be enriched, as you find your heart and mind challenged by saints from across the last two centuries and even earlier. Dr. Leslie Wilcox observed the powerful impact such reading can have—an influence akin to that of a close relationship:

> Reading establishes a friendship. It may be with someone you never see or someone who lived long ago, but if you think much with them, there is an intellectual friendship set up with them. As an example, the first book I ever read that was written by Daniel Steele was *Love Enthroned*, which I first obtained and read in 1928 or 1929. It is an excellent book on holiness. Through the next twenty years I obtained and read several more of his books. They have become some of the most treasured volumes in my library and have influenced my thinking very strongly. I

never met the man but he has had an influence upon my life almost equal to a personal friendship.[69]

In addition, what would be a better time than this season of commemoration to share Holiness books with others? Who knows but what this will foster a new revival of holiness in our own time, much like that in which Martin Wells Knapp participated and of which he acknowledged, "Much of the success of the great Full Salvation Movement, which is belting the globe to-day, is due to the faithful circulation of good books, and the further spread of this movement, and its preservation from error, is conditioned largely upon the same thing."[70] May we each do our part to preserve and promulgate the message of holiness today.

---

69. From an early catalog of Schmul Publishing Company.
70. Seth C. Rees, et. al. *Pentecostal Messengers* (Cincinnati: M. W. Knapp, 1898), 70.

THE CHRISTIAN'S MANUAL,

A TREATISE ON CHRISTIAN PERFECTION; WITH DIRECTIONS FOR OBTAINING THAT STATE.

Compiled Principally From the Works of the Rev. John Wesley

by

The Rev. T. Merritt

Publisher's Preface

THE NAME OF TIMOTHY Merritt has almost passed from the memory of Holiness people, yet in his day, he exerted a tremendous influence upon society and the church around him. Born at the outset of the American Revolution to a Connecticut family of Puritan heritage, he was converted in 1792, and entered the ministry four years later.

Years later, he wrote the book now before you, and a nineteen-year-old girl picked it up in 1825— Sarah Lankford. *The Christian's Manual* exerted such an effect upon her that she resolved to enter the blessing of Perfect Love, and three months later she obtained her desire.

In 1835, Sarah Lankford had the opportunity to return grace for grace when she founded the famous Tuesday Meetings for the Promotion of Holiness. At the very first of these meetings, Timothy Merritt's wife was present.

> Another, and another, and yet another testified— "Jesus saves me this afternoon as never before." Our beloved sister Merritt, wife of Rev. Timothy Merritt, said, "For thirty years I have been a seeker. This afternoon Christ is *my* savior. Never before could I say

it without fear. Now I rest upon Christ as I do upon my chair, without fear of falling."[71]

The Tuesday Meetings were not met with great approval by Sarah's sister, Phoebe Palmer, but Sarah soon led her into the experience of sanctification. Phoebe Palmer went on to become known as the Mother of the Holiness Movement. Thus, Timothy Merritt's *The Christian's Manual* affected thousands in the following decades, right up to the present day.

---

71. George Hughes, *Fragrant Memories* (Salem, OH: Schmul Publishing Co., 1988), 12.

Preface.

SOME YEARS AGO IT occurred to my mind that it might be a useful labour to furnish, in a small cheap form, directions for such Christians as are convinced of the attainableness of Christian perfection, and are *desirous* to obtain it. Such often meet with difficulties, and need a guide. To furnish one which they may always carry with them, is the design of the following compilation. I say compilation; for much of the following pages is found in the writings of those excellent men, *Wesley* and *Fletcher*. Should any object to my making a book, in part, out of the writings of others, my answer is, 1. Mr. Wesley himself often did this. 2. What I have brought together in the following compendium, is, in its original form, dispersed through several volumes, which many persons have neither time to read, nor money to purchase.

The design of this little manual was formed and the work commenced some years ago: but a sense of the want of ability for such a work, caused it to be delayed from time to time, and now it goes to the public with many imperfections, as every thing must that goes from the hand of so weak an instrument.

As the work was written at intervals of considerable distance from each other, there may not be found that uniformity of style and expression, which leisure to transcribe might have given to it.

At the suggestion of a judicious friend I have prefixed a short chapter upon justification, that the serious reader may have a view of the whole subject. The observations and directions at the end of the 4th chapter were suggested by the same friend. The "Reflections designed as Helps to a Growth in Grace," at the end of the book, are original, and from the pen of a female correspondent of the author's.

T. M.

Bristol, R. I. April 8th, 1824.

Chapter I.
The Necessity and Nature of Justification.

THE SCRIPTURES INFORM US that "God created man in his own image," a holy and happy being. But it is very manifest that he has lost his innocency and happiness and has become guilty and wretched. This is the character which the Scriptures give to mankind universally. And it necessarily follows, that if men are fallen creatures, their actions, till they are renewed, must be sinful; and if sinful, they are wretched beyond description.

In this state were all mankind when "God so loved the world that he gave his only begotten Son; that whosoever believeth in him should not perish, but have everlasting life." As guilty, man must be pardoned. As polluted, and possessing a mind which is enmity against God, he must be renewed. The former of these changes is called *justification*, the latter *sanctification*.

There is not only a difference between justification and sanctification in their essential nature, but there is this farther difference, that our pardon is full, our justification is complete, as having respect to *all* our past sins:

but our sanctification at *that* time is ordinarily only in *part*. It is of the latter of these that I principally treat in the following essay. At present, however, I would speak briefly of the former, namely, of justification.

Justification is preceded by the illumination of the understanding whereby the sinner is convinced of the corruption of his nature and the sinfulness of his life. If he has been moral, and observed the outward duties of religion, when he comes to receive the true light he sees himself a sinner, and that he has in all things come short of the glory of God. With this discovery there is usually a great degree of unbelief and slavish fear which darken the soul, and keep the gospel method of salvation out of sight. And here we have continual evidence of the utter inability of any human being to teach man wisdom; for though the awakened sinner be told repeatedly, and in the plainest manner, that Christ has made an atonement for his sins, and that he may be saved by grace through faith in that atonement, and can be saved in no other way; he seldom yields to this method, though it be near at hand, till he has tried the virtue of his own righteousness, and found by experience that it is insufficient to justify him before God. These efforts to save himself do but protract the period of his deliverance from condemnation and wrath. They also serve to perplex his mind, to make him scruple the depth and genuineness of his repentance, to hide the mercy of God from his view, and fill his soul with horrible forebodings of eternal ruin. At length, finding no good thing in himself, and finding his own efforts utterly unavailing, he is driven by the necessity of his case, to give himself up, and to trust alone in the mercy of the Saviour; and in doing so he finds *rest to his soul*. This is the first act of submission to the will of God, and affiance in his mercy; and is immediately followed by an act of acceptance on the part of God. Soon, and in general immediately, but perhaps not always, the Spirit bears witness with his spirit that he is a child of God; that he is pardoned and adopted for Christ's sake. Instantly his heart dissolves in love and thankfulness, and he cries out, *My Lord and my God.* He feels that a great change is wrought not only in his external relations, but *in* him, in the frame of his mind, and the dispositions of his soul; delivering him from the spirit of bondage and fear; changing the heart of stone into a heart of flesh, and shedding abroad therein the love of God and man. He feels that he is a new creature, and exults in his happy change. "Being justified by faith he has peace with God, through our Lord Jesus Christ." Having the Spirit of adoption, *he rejoices with joy unspeakable and full of glory.*

This is the ordinary experience and portion of the new born soul. But there are many instances of persons who have been truly awakened, and have fled for refuge and laid hold on the hope set before them, who have not had so clear an evidence of their acceptance in Christ, and who, of course, have had little or no joy. But it is essential to our being children of God, in the lowest sense, that we have faith in Christ and victory over sin. Faith, in the lowest sense, being a trust in Christ, implies our submission to him, and acceptance of him as our Saviour; and while our wills are thus given up to him, they are not employed against him, and indeed cannot be. And this explains the words of St. John, *He that is born of God cannot commit sin* — his will cannot be exerted in contrary ways at the same time; and hence it would seem that peace with God and peace of conscience are the necessary and inseparable fruits of faith. But we cannot say the same of all the sensible comforts of grace, particularly of *joy.* This is not the inseparable fruit of faith, because faith is often found without it. The fruit of faith, like the fruit of a tree, may be partially hindered even when the stock is good.

But the feeble Christian who has not received the clear and abiding witness of the Spirit, should be taught to ask for it, and encouraged to expect this great privilege of the children of God. And he has a right to expect it, according to many promises, especially that emphatically called by our Saviour *the promise of the Father*, that is, the promise of the Holy Ghost as a comforter to dwell in all true believers.

But the grand error of many Christians is, as soon as they obtain what is called "a hope," to stop there and look no farther. The unavoidable consequence of this is, that they soon lose ground; the eye of their soul is darkened, the ardour of their desires is abated, the warmth of their affection in some measure cooled, leanness comes into their souls, and in a little time the corruptions of their hearts spring up again and prevail over them. Thus are they brought into a more grievous bondage than that from which they had so lately escaped.

But should it be otherwise with such a one, and should he stand fast in the liberty wherewith Christ has made him free, he will sooner or later feel the need of a deeper work of grace. He will find indeed that he is sanctified but in *part*.

Let him not at this time of trial cast away his confidence, which *has great recompense of reward*. It may appear at times a desperate attempt to believe and hope against so many trials, and so great unlikeness to God as he finds in himself. Still let him hope against hope. Let him cast his care upon his God, and wait patiently for him, and he shall find in the end that it is not a vain thing to trust in the Lord in the darkest hour. He shall come out of the furnace more pure than he went in. He does not merely hold his own, but he grows in grace and in the knowledge of our Lord Jesus Christ. Thus if he stand fast in the time of trial, and is at all times found pressing forward, he shall attain unto all the mind that was in Christ, and shall grow up to the measure of the stature of the fulness of Christ.

Chapter II.
Of Christian Perfection.

HAVING OBSERVED IN THE foregoing chapter that Christians may go on to perfection, it may not be amiss in this place to show more particularly in what respects they may be perfect.

1. "Christians are not perfect in knowledge: they are not *so* perfect in this life, as to be free from ignorance.

"Innumerable are the things they know not. Touching the Almighty himself, they cannot search him out to perfection. Neither is it for them to know the times and seasons when God will work his great work upon the earth;" no, nor when the coming of the Son of man shall be. "They know not the reasons even of many of his dispensations with the sons of men: but are constrained to rest here. Though clouds and darkness are round about him, righteousness and judgment are the habitation of his throne. And how little do they know of what is ever before them, even of the visible works of his hands. How "he spreadeth the north over the empty place, and hangeth the earth upon nothing." How he uniteth all the parts of this vast machine by a secret chain which cannot be broken. So great is the ignorance, so very little the knowledge, of even the best of men!

2. "As no one is so perfect as to be free from ignorance, so neither from mistake, which indeed is almost an unavoidable consequence of it. It is true the children of God do not mistake as to the things essential to salvation, for they are *taught of God;* and the way which he teacheth them, the way of holiness, is so plain, that 'the wayfaring man, though a fool, need not err therein.' But in things unessential to salvation, they do err, and that frequently. The best and wisest of men are frequently mistaken even with respect to facts; believing those things not to have been, which really were, or those to have been done which were not." Hence also they may mistake the actions and the characters of men, believing some to be either better or worse than they are, and others to be good when they are bad, or bad when they are good.

"Nay, with regard to the Holy Scriptures themselves, the best of men are liable to mistake: especially with respect to those parts thereof, which less immediately relate to practice."

3. We may add, Christians are not free from infirmities in this life. "I mean hereby, not those which are properly termed *bodily infirmities*, but all those inward or outward imperfections, which are not of a moral nature. Such as weakness or slowness of understanding, dullness or confusedness of apprehension, incoherency of thought, irregular quickness or heaviness of imagination, the want of a ready or retentive memory. Such also are slowness of speech, impropriety of language, and ungracefulness of pronunciation; to which one might add a thousand nameless defects, either in conversation or behaviour. From these none

can hope to be perfectly freed till the spirit return to God who gave it.

4. "Neither can we expect, till then, to be wholly free from temptation." The Son of God was tempted in the days of his flesh, and it is enough for the servant to be as his Master.

5. "Christian perfection, therefore, does not imply an exemption either from ignorance, or mistake, or infirmities, or temptations. Indeed, it is only another term for holiness. And everyone that is holy, is, in the Scripture sense, perfect. Yet we may lastly observe, that neither in this respect is there any absolute perfection on earth. — There is no perfection *of degrees;* — none which does not admit of a continual increase. So that how much soever any man has attained, or in how high a degree soever he is perfect, he hath still need to *grow in grace,* and daily to advance in the knowledge and love of God."*

Wherein then, it may be asked, does Christian perfection consist? It consists, first, in being delivered from the power of sin so as not to *commit* sin. "The Word of God plainly declares, that those who are born again, even in the lowest sense, do not continue in sin; that they cannot *live any longer therein,* Rom. vi,1,2; that they are planted together in the likeness of Christ's death, that their 'old man is crucified with him, the body of sin being destroyed, so that henceforth they do not serve sin; that being dead with Christ, they are freed from sin,' that they are 'dead unto sin, and alive unto God,' that 'sin hath no more dominion over them,' who are 'not under the law, but under grace;' but that these 'being free from sin, are become the servants of righteousness,'" 5-18.

St. Peter expresses the same thing: "He that hath suf-

---

*Wesley's sermons on Christian perfection: and the following quotations in this chapter are from the same.

fered in the flesh hath ceased from sin,— that he no longer should live to the desires of men, but to the will of God," 1 Pet. iv, 1, 2. St. John says, "He that committeth sin is of the devil. For this purpose the Son of God was manifested, that he might destroy the works of the devil. Whosoever is born of God doth not commit sin," &c, 1 John iii, 4-10.

"Secondly, This perfection implies a deliverance from evil thoughts and evil tempers. First, from evil or sinful thoughts. But here let it be observed, that thoughts concerning evil are not always evil thoughts. A man, for instance, may think of a murder which another has committed, and yet this is no evil or sinful thought. So our blessed Lord himself doubtless thought of, or understood, the thing spoken by the devil, when he said, 'All this will I give thee, if thou wilt fall down and worship me.' Yet had he no evil or sinful thoughts, nor indeed was capable of any, because his will was always right with the will of his Father. And hence it follows, that neither have any real Christians sinful thoughts. 'For everyone that is perfect is as his Master,' Luke vi, 40. Indeed, a thousand thoughts which are raised in our minds by outward objects, or by the injections of the devil, are evil: in one sense they are troublesome, but they are not sinful while they have no concurrence of the will, and the heart remains right with God. Sinful thoughts proceed out of a sinful heart: if therefore the heart be made good, the thoughts will be good also." (See Mark vii, 21 and 2 Cor. x, 4, 5, &c.)

Thirdly, Christians may be cleansed from those sinful tempers which remain in the heart after justification. Yea, they may be cleansed from *all sin, from all filthiness of flesh and spirit;* from all desire or self will; from all pride, anger, impatience, and the like; so that no root of bitterness or sin, nothing to mar our peace or grieve the Holy Spirit, shall be found in us. *Old things shall all be done away, and all things become new.* We may be sanctified wholly, according to the prayer of the apostle. — 1 Thess. v, 23.

But all this would not be enough if it were not accompanied, lastly, with all the *fulness of God.* It would not be enough to be cleansed from sin, but we must be filled with the positive fruits of the Spirit, the mind that was in Christ.

This we are assured we may receive. Our bodies shall *so* become the temples of the Holy Ghost, that God, the Father, Son, and Holy Ghost, shall *live in us and walk in us.* The kingdom of God, which is righteousness, peace, and joy in the Holy Ghost, shall *so* be set up in us as to bring all into subjection unto God. We shall every one be able to say with St. Paul, "I am crucified with Christ: nevertheless I live; yet not I, but Christ liveth in me: and the life I now live, I live by faith in the Son of God, who loved me and gave himself for me," Gal. ii, 20.

Such a one loves the Lord his God with all his heart, and soul, and mind, and strength, and his neighbour as himself. — God is his only object and aim; and he finds in him all that he needs, even righteousness, strength, and peace. All tormenting fear is banished from his mind, and the Spirit itself beareth witness with his spirit that he is a child of God, wholly sanctified and set apart for God. As the work commenced, and was carried on and accomplished through faith, so by faith he holds it fast; for it is by faith he walks, by faith he stands, and by faith he lives, even by that *faith which is the substance of things hoped for, the evidence of things not seen.*

Having stated the doctrine of Christian perfection, and shown what we may, and what we may not, expect to be delivered from in this life; it may not be amiss to produce some of the proofs of this doctrine. I say some of the proofs: for it is not my intention to go largely into the subject, but merely to say enough to satisfy the sincere inquirers after truth.

1. We prove the doctrine of Christian perfection from the character of God, and the relation we stand in to him. God is holy, — he is infinitely just and good. He never willed that men should sin; nor can he look upon the depravity of their hearts any more than upon the sinfulness of their lives, but with compassion for their souls, and abhorrence of their sin and uncleanness. He must, from the essential holiness of his nature, require holiness of all his moral creatures. *He requireth truth in the inward parts—* the truth or substance of his own law written upon their hearts and printed in their thoughts. He can no more approve an unholy desire or temper, than the act of adultery or murder.

2. God has clearly and fully expressed his will in the law he has given to us; and this law is the standard of Christian perfection. He says, *Be ye holy, for I am holy*, 1 Pet. i, 16. *Follow peace with all men, and holiness without which no man shall see the Lord,* Heb. xii, 15. *Be ye perfect, even as your Father who is in heaven is perfect,* Matt. v, 48. *Thou shalt love the Lord thy God with all thy heart, and with all thy soul, and with all thy strength, and with all thy mind, and thy neighbour as thyself,* Luke x, 27. This *love is the fulfilling of the law*; for where love *fills* the heart, there can be no sin, but every good temper, word, and work.

3. God not only requires holiness of us, but he has made provision in the Gospel that *we may fulfill all righteousness. For what the law could not do, in that it was weak through the flesh, God hath done by sending his own Son in the likeness of sinful flesh, and for sin condemned sin in the flesh; that the righteousness of the law might be fulfilled in us, who walk not after the flesh, but after the*

Spirit, Rom. viii, 3, 4. Our own darkness, weakness, and sinfulness, can be no objection; for *Jesus Christ is made unto us wisdom, righteousness, sanctification and redemption,* 1 Cor. i, 30.

The most abundant provision is made in the gospel for us. Yes,

"In Christ all fulness dwells,
And for all wretched man."

His blood atones for our sins; his merit obtains for us both grace and glory. He has opened a fountain, in which we may wash and be clean, both from the guilt of actual sin, and from the remains of the carnal mind; and he has procured the Holy Spirit to enlighten our minds, to renew us after the image of God, and fill us with all the fruits of righteousness. The means which God has provided are every way equal to the end to be accomplished.

4. But as though this were not enough, he has condescended to make particular and special promises to cleanse us from all sin, and perfect us in holiness. "Unto us are given exceeding great and precious promises; that by these ye might be partakers of the divine nature, having escaped the corruption that is in the world through lust," 2 Pet. i, 4. And these promises are generally more full and explicit than those relating to any other subject. Thus, in Ezekiel, "Then will I sprinkle clean water upon you, and ye shall be *clean,* from *all* your filthiness and from *all* your idols will I *cleanse you,*" Ezek. xxxvi, 25, 26. Thus St. John, "If we walk in the light, as he is in the light, we have fellowship one with another, and the blood of Jesus Christ his Son cleanseth us from *all sin.* If we confess our sins, he is faithful and just to forgive us our sins, and to cleanse us from *all* unrighteousness," 1 John i, 7,9. To the same purpose is that ancient promise recorded by Moses. "And the Lord thy God will *circumcise thine heart,* and the

heart of thy seed, to love the Lord thy God with *all* thy heart, and with *all* thy soul, that thou mayest live," Deut. xxx, 6. And we may truly say that whatever the law of God requires, the gospel promises, in that it engages that the law shall be *put into our minds,* and written *in our hearts*— that is, whatever the law requires shall be fully accomplished in them that believe, Heb. viii, 10. The Gospel, as containing all good things for us, is by way of eminence called *the promise*; and we are assured that "no good thing shall be withholden from them that walk uprightly," Psa. lxxxiv, 11. Having given us his well-beloved "Son, how shall he not with him also freely give us all things?" Rom. viii, 32. And this above all, *holiness of heart?* If there be one thing that God is more willing to give us than another, it is *holiness*. This, therefore, is contained as well in the promises of the gospel, as in the precepts of the law. And what God has promised we may certainly expect. His promise cannot fail. If he had promised to give us freedom from all human infirmities in this life, we might look for this also. But this he has not done, and therefore no one looks for it. But he has promised us the full and complete sanctification of our nature; and this therefore we may obtain.

5. Those who live in sin dishonour God, but such as turn from their sins, and work righteousness, glorify him. And as some of the wicked dishonour him more than others, so some of the righteous honour him more than others, and they who are the most like him, that have the most of his image, of his Spirit, and grace, glorify him the most. We shall never glorify him fully, in our full measure, till we are wholly sanctified; till our pride, selfwill, and all the angry passions, are destroyed, and our repentance, faith, and love, are perfected, and our hearts and lives such as the gospel requires. If therefore we would glorify God, we should *perfect holiness in the fear of God.*

6. We may go farther still, and say, if Christians would not backslide, and bring reproach upon the cause of Christ, they must *go on to perfection*. There is no medium between going forward and drawing back. As soon as any one ceases to press forwards, he declines in spiritual life; and if he does not discover it, and return to God, his love soon grows cold, he loses his strength, and backsliding little by little, at length becomes an apostate from the faith. Or, if he does not wholly apostatize, yet he loses the enjoyment of religion, and drags on heavily. He neglects his duty, and becomes worldly minded. Sinful desires, tempers, and passions spring up within him, and he is brought into the most uncomfortable and cruel bondage. In this state he can neither serve God nor his brethren.

On the other hand, he that walks in Christ as he has received him, and goes on adding to his faith, virtue, knowledge[,] temperance, patience, godliness, brotherly kindness, and charity, "shall be neither barren nor unfruitful in the knowledge of our Lord and Saviour Jesus Christ." And though he does not yet obtain deliverance from all the remains of the carnal mind, yet he "grows in grace, and his path shall shine more and more unto the perfect day."

7. We may add, in the last place, that this state has been actually attained by the saints in every age, according to their respective dispensations. Job was *perfect and upright*. Noah was perfect in his generation: Caleb and Joshua *fully followed the Lord*. Isaiah had his *iniquity taken away, and his sin purged*. But it is chiefly in the New Testament that we are to look for examples of this great salvation. And of this character were all those who were "filled with faith and the Holy Ghost" — those to whom the apostle speaks, "Let as many of us as be perfect be thus minded" — those called by the same apostle "holy breth-

ren" — and finally, all those of whom St. John says, "As he (Christ) is, so are we in this world."

Thus it appears that the doctrine of full sanctification, or Christian perfection, may be as easily proved as any other doctrine of the Bible. While the law, which is the will of God, makes it our *duty* to be holy; the gospel, with its grace and promises, *secures* it to us.

This must be infinitely desirable to every one who has reflected upon the subject. It is desirable that we may be wholly pleasing to God, that we may glorify him fully in our bodies and spirits which are his. It is desirable on our own account; for this

> ["]Lays the rough path of peevish nature even,
> And opens in each breast a little heaven."

While it brings perfect resignation and union to God, it yields abundance of peace and assurance forever. It is equally desirable for Christians as members of society; for were all sinful desires and tempers destroyed, and did love to God and man fill the heart, there would be no more wars and fightings, no more brother going to law with brother before the unjust, no more broils and contentions, no more strife of tongues, no more coldness and distance of affection between brethren, no looking on their own things merely; but that love which seeketh not her own— which ["]believeth all things, hopeth all things, endureth all things, and never faileth," would introduce universal peace and happiness.

> "Happy the souls that thus believe,
> To Jesus and each other cleave;
> Join'd by the unction from above,
> In mystic fellowship of love."

Then we might sing,
> "Bless'd are the sons of peace,
> Whose hearts and hopes are one,

Whose kind designs to serve and please,
   Through all their actions run.

"As on the heavenly hills,
   The saints are bless'd above;
Their joy like morning dew distills,
   And all the air is love."

It may be proper, before I close this chapter, just to notice two or three objections which otherwise might perplex the young inquirer, and hinder his progress in sanctification.

1. An objection to our sanctification is often taken from the moral condition of men, as fallen creatures. It is said that we are such ignorant, weak, depraved and miserable creatures, that any kind of perfection is impossible for us.

Answer. It would be impossible if we were required to make *ourselves* perfect. This is not the case. The mighty God is our Saviour. And what can be too hard for the Almighty? Is his hand shortened that it cannot save? Nay, but he can still do all things — all things that are agreeable to his will. And we have seen that this is his will, to save his people from *all* their sins. This then should satisfy us. For though God can do nothing against his own will, yet whatever is agreeable to his will, he can certainly accomplish. And when it is said that this or that is his will, we must understand that it is infinitely agreeable to him. "Behold what manner of love the Father hath bestowed upon us, that we should be called the children of God." And has he not power to make us what he would have us to be? Yes, verily, we may say, "If thou wilt, thou canst make us clean." What cannot infinite love effect! Let us then cast ourselves on the love of God. Let us put our trust in the Lord Jesus Christ. Let us yield to the drawings of the Holy Spirit, and all is ours: his wisdom and knowledge, his mercy and truth, his power and grace, are ours.

2. A second objection here is built on some few passages of Scripture which are thought to contradict this doctrine. Solomon says, "There is no man that sinneth not," 1 Kings viii, 46; 2 Chron. vi, 36; yea, "there is not a just man upon earth that doeth good, and sinneth not," Eccles. vii, 20.

Answer. If we were to allow that thus it was from Adam to Christ, that the best of men did perform some actions, which, according to the strictness of the law, had sin in them; yet it will not follow that under the gospel this must be the case. "The privileges of Christians are in no wise to be measured by what the Old Testament records concerning those who were under the Jewish dispensation, seeing the fulness of time is now come; the Holy Ghost is now given; the great salvation of God is brought unto men, by the revelation of Jesus Christ. The kingdom of heaven is now set up on earth: concerning which the Spirit of God declared of old, 'He that is feeble among them (believers under the Gospel) at that day'— the gospel day in which we live, 'shall be as David; and the house of David shall be as God, as the angel of the Lord before them.' More light and grace are given under the Gospel than were ever enjoyed before; so that the least Christian is greater than John the Baptist, or any that went before him."

But it will, perhaps, be urged, that the New Testament declares that "if we say we have no sin, we deceive ourselves," 1 John i, 8.

"I answer, 1," says Mr. Wesley, "The tenth verse fixes the sense of the eighth: 'If we say we have no sin,' in the former, being explained by, 'If we say we have not sinned,' in the latter verse: 2. The point under consideration is not whether we have, or have not, sinned *heretofore;* and neither of these verses assert that we do sin or commit sin *now:* 3. The ninth verse explains both the eighth and tenth. 'If we confess our sins, he is faithful and just to forgive us our sins, and to cleanse us from all unrighteousness.'"

It may be thought that the case described in the seventh chapter of Romans affords an argument against the doctrine of full sanctification in this life.

Let it be observed that the apostle, in that chapter, personifies one under conviction, and not one who is made free by Christ, as all true believers are. This is evident from the scope and design of the apostle's argument. He first shows *how* he was convinced of sin, namely, by the law. In the next place he describes his internal exercises while under conviction. Here we find that his mind being enlightened, his conscience and will sided with the law, though that condemned him. In this condition he would fain have cast off sin, and performed every good deed; but not having received Christ by faith, he was continually brought into bondage to the *law,* or power of *sin in his members.* Hereupon he cried out,"O wretched man that I am! who shall deliver me from this body of death?" Rom. vii, 24. In that moment it was given him to see whence deliverance was to come, namely, *through Jesus Christ our Lord;* and, laying hold on the hope set before him, he realized deliverance, and immediately broke out in the language of exultation, saying, "There is therefore now no condemnation to them that are in Christ Jesus, who walk not after the flesh but after the Spirit. For the law of the spirit of life in Christ Jesus hath made me free from the law of sin and death," Rom. viii, 1,2.

Thus it appears that these texts afford no support to the objection; but are perfectly consistent with the doctrine of salvation from all sin.

3. The last objection I shall notice is taken from the supposed benefit of having some sin remain in us. This, it is said, will keep us humble— will endear Christ to us, and cause us to hunger and thirst after righteousness.

Answer. 1. Does not this objection involve the principle so severely reprobated by the apostle, "Let us do evil that good may come,"— let some sin remain to keep us humble, &c, "whose damnation," says he, "is just."

2. Those who bring this objection appear not to consider the absurdity it contains. Did anyone ever suppose that *sickness* produces *health?* That *darkness* produces *light* or *weakness, strength?* And yet this would not be more absurd than to suppose that *sin* can produce humility, and make us hunger and thirst after righteousness! No, sin *never* produces these effects, but quite the contrary. It does not make us more humble, but more proud. It does not endear Christ to us, but renders our hearts cold towards him. It does not cause us to hunger and thirst after righteousness, but dims our spiritual sight, weakens our desires after holiness, shakes good resolutions, slackens our pace, and produces unspeakable mischief.

The experience of every Christian will refute this objection. Every Christian knows that when he had more sin than he now has, he was more proud, had less love to Christ, and less hunger and thirst after righteousness: and also that the more holy desires and affections prevail, the more he hates and dreads sin, and ardently desires to be freed from all sin, and made conformable to the image of God. And it may safely be said that none are so penitent and humble, none value Christ so high, none admire the beauties of holiness so much, as those who are saved from all sin.

We shall never hate sin with a perfect hatred, nor love God with a perfect love, till we are sanctified wholly, till we can say with the apostle, "I am crucified with Christ:

nevertheless, I live; yet not I, but Christ liveth in me; and the life I now live, I live by the faith of the Son of God, who loved me, and gave himself for me," Gal. ii, 20.

Chapter III.
Directions for Seeking Christian Perfection.

1. IF A MAN WOULD hit a mark, he must know where it is; otherwise, he will be likely to shoot above or below it, on this side or on that. If anyone would seek sanctification or Christian perfection (for I use these terms as synonymous in this treatise), he must know what it is; for if he include in his view of it either more or less than God has required and promised, he is seeking something beside the thing itself and cannot succeed. "Some people," says Mr. Fletcher, "aim at Christian perfection, but mistaking angelical perfection for it, they shoot above the mark, miss it, and then peevishly give up their hopes. Others place the mark as much too low. Hence it is that you hear them profess to have attained Christian perfection when they have not so much as attained the mental serenity of a philosopher, or the candor of a good-natured, conscientious heathen." And I add after him, in the preceding pages, if I am not mistaken, the mark is fixed according to the rules of Scriptural moderation. It is not placed so high as to make you despair of hitting it, if you do your best in a gospel

way: nor yet so low as to allow you to presume that you can reach it without exerting all your abilities to the uttermost, in due subordination to the efficacy of Jesus's blood, and the Spirit's sanctifying influence.

It is not the perfection of angels, nor yet that of Adam before he fell, that is required of Christians; but it is a greater degree of perfection than was required of the heathen, or even of the Jews under the Mosaic dispensation. If you would know exactly what it is, you must look into the gospel to find it. It is neither more nor less than what God has commanded and promised. This does not imply that we know every thing; that we shall never mistake, never err, &c. But it does imply that we are saved from all perverseness and stubbornness of our will, and hardness of heart; from every wrong desire, and sinful temper; and that we love God with all the heart, and our neighbour as ourselves. In a word, this perfection consists in the absence of all sin, properly so called, and in being filled with the fruits of righteousness, humility, repentance, faith, love, meekness, patience, and whatever is implied in Christian holiness.

2. It is not less necessary to be deeply impressed with the importance of this state, than to have clear ideas of it. Many have clear ideas of the doctrines of the gospel, of the way of life and salvation by Christ Jesus, who, nevertheless, never feel their importance, who never receive Christ as their Saviour. In like manner many Christians acknowledge the doctrine of sanctification, who feel not the importance of it, and of course make no vigorous efforts to obtain it.

Mr. Wesley says, "There have been from the beginning two orders of Christians. The one lived an innocent life, conforming, in all things not sinful, to the customs and fashions of the world, doing many good works, abstaining from gross evils, and attending the ordinances of God. They endeavoured in general to have a conscience void of offense in their behavior, but did not aim at any particular strictness, being in most things like their neighbours. The other Christians not only abstained from all appearance of evil, were zealous of good works in every kind, and attended all the ordinances of God; but likewise used all diligence to attain all the mind that was in Christ, and laboured to walk, in every point, as their beloved Master. In order to do this, they walked in a constant course of universal self denial, trampling on every pleasure which they were not divinely conscious prepared them for taking pleasure in God. They took up their cross daily. They strove, they agonized without intermission, to enter in at the strait gate. This one thing they did; they spared no pains to arrive at the summit of Christian holiness: leaving the first principles of the doctrine of Christ to go on to perfection: to know all that love of God which passeth knowledge, and to be filled with all the fulness of God.

"From long experience and observation," continues Mr. Wesley, "I am inclined to think, that whoever finds redemption in the blood of Jesus, whoever is justified, has then the choice of walking in the higher or the lower path. I believe the Holy Spirit at that time sets before him the more excellent way, and incites him to walk herein, to choose the narrowest path in the narrow way, to aspire after the heights and depths of holiness, after the entire image of God. But if he does not accept this offer, he insensibly declines into the lower order of Christians. He still goes on, perhaps, in what may be called a good way, serving God in his degree, and finds mercy in the close of life, through the blood of the covenant." But it is a great wonder, and a miracle of mercy, if he stops at the lower order of Christians, if he does not fall again into the spirit of the world, and *lose his soul.*

Allowing that he might save his soul, that he preserves just religion enough to screen him from wrath in the great and terrible day of the Lord; yet what Christian can feel content with just so much and no more?

"Thus much I affirm," says the author last quoted, "they will not have so high a place in heaven as they would have had, if they had chosen the better path: and will this be a small loss? The having so many fewer stars in the crown of your glory! Will it be a little thing to have a lower place than you might have had in the kingdom of your Father? Certainly there will be no sorrow in heaven: there all tears shall be wiped from our eyes. But if it were possible grief could enter there, we should grieve at the irreparable loss! Irreparable then, but not now! Now, by the grace of God, we may choose the *more excellent way.*"

It shall not only be to our advantage in the future state, but also while we are here upon earth, to be holy in heart and life. — Holiness is in some sense its own reward. The suitableness and fitness of it, in all respects, render it the most desirable thing in the world, and when possessed, yields the greatest delight to the soul. Yes, the fruit of holiness is "peace that passeth all understanding, and joy unspeakable and full of glory." It is given to such, and to such only, to "rejoice evermore, pray without ceasing, and in all things to give thanks." Every Christian, even the babe in Christ, knows there is no happiness like that of communion and fellowship with God; and when this divine enjoyment is interrupted, he goes mourning all the day, and refuses to be comforted by any thing, till he finds his beloved. Who then can tell the joy that would result from having him always with you, ruling and keeping your heart! What ineffable delight must flow from the closest walk with him, from knowing that all your ways please him, from being cleansed from all sin, and wholly devoted to his will! This is a sort of heaven on earth.

This is not all. The sanctified Christian is much more useful than he could otherwise be. He is a light shining in a dark place. His spirit and conversation operate like leaven upon those about him. No idle words proceed out of his mouth, no vain, filthy, or injurious conversation; but only that which is *good to the use of edifying*. He adorns the gospel of God his Saviour in all things, and recommends piety to all about him.

But the object which lies nearest the heart of the Christian is the glory of God. While we lived in sin we dishonoured God: and we glorify him only so far as we are like him. But the sanctified Christian is wholly devoted to God, and therefore "glorifies God in his body and spirit which are God's. He is crucified with Christ, yea, he lives not, but Christ liveth in him. He walketh as Christ walked. He has the mind that was in Christ." His will is so resigned that he can say, "not my will, but *thine be done.*" He obeys cheerfully, and suffers patiently, all this will. His life and actions show that God is "the strength of his heart, and his portion for ever." He shows that rare and happy consistency between the profession and practice of holiness, while he gives proof that he is a "stranger and pilgrim on the earth, and that his affections are set on things above."

Now if you would successfully seek sanctification you must get your mind deeply impressed with the importance of that blessing. Survey its magnitude; consider how essential it is for your own greater happiness here and hereafter. Consider its connexion with the best interests of your fellow creatures. But above all, consider it as connected with the glory of God; and you will see, you will *feel* its importance. You cannot entertain low thoughts of it — you cannot feel indifferent towards it. And if Christian holiness will make you more happy, render you more useful, and enable you to glorify God in a higher degree than you could possibly do without it, you will feel it your indispensable *duty* to seek it, and not give up the pursuit till you obtain it? [sic]

3. When the mind is deeply impressed with the importance of sanctification and the entire devotion of the heart and life to God, let an intention to this effect take place in the mind; let a firm resolution be formed to devote the whole heart and life to God, to go on to perfection. We never accomplish any business, we never take a journey, we never rise up or sit down, till the mind resolves to do so.

A man may know that such a piece of work ought to be done; he may think how much to his advantage it would be to have it accomplished; and he may sincerely and earnestly desire to perform it. But after all, if he does not resolve upon it and actually set about it, he will never see it accomplished. It is thus with respect to justification. Many are called by the awakening Spirit of God and have good desires for religion: but they never resolve on turning to God; they never actually set about seeking the salvation of their souls; and of course they stand where they are till they lose all their good desires, and are carried away again by the strong current of their earthly desires and sinful passions. But others, seeing their danger, and knowing what they want, resolve to give up all for Christ, and soon obtain rest for their souls. In like manner, such as see the necessity of sanctification, and resolve to seek it in the appointed way, and actually set about it, and press forward, soon obtain it. But without this resolution nothing can be done.

"Set out," says Mr. Fletcher, "for the Canaan of perfect love with a firm resolution to labour for the rest which remains on earth for the people of God. Your good resolutions need not fail: nor will they fail, if, under a due sense of the fickleness and helplessness of your unassisted free will, you properly depend upon God's faithfulness and assistance. However, should they fail, as they probably will do more than once, be not discouraged, but repent, search out the cause, and in the strength of free grace, let your assisted free will renew your evangelical purpose, till the Lord seals it with his mighty fiat, and says, 'Let it be done according to thy resolving faith.' Should it be suggested to you that such a resolution would be presumption, you may repel the temptation by the many examples recorded in the Bible. The prodigal son said, 'I will arise and go to my father.' David said, 'I will love thee, O Lord my God: — I will behold thy face in righteousness: — I am purposed that my mouth shall not transgress: — I will keep it as with a bridle: — I have said, that I would keep thy word: — The proud have had me exceedingly in derision, but I will keep thy precepts with my *whole heart*. I have sworn and I will perform it, that I will keep thy righteous judgments.' Jacob said, 'I will not let thee go, except thou bless me;' Gen. xxxii, 26, and Paul, 'I am determined not to know any thing among you save Jesus Christ, and him crucified.'"

"Much diligence," says Kempis, "is necessary to him that would profit much. If he who firmly purposeth, often faileth, what shall he do who seldom or feebly purposeth any thing?"

Let me strengthen these observations by one from Mr. Law. "It was this general purpose that made the primitive Christians such eminent instances of piety. And if you will here stop, and ask yourself why you are not so pious as the primitive Christians were, your own heart will tell you, it is neither through ignorance nor inability, but purely because you never thoroughly intended it. You observe the same Sunday worship that they did, and you are strict in it, because it is your full intention to be so. And when you as fully intend to be like them in their common life; when you intend to please God in all your actions, you will find it as possible to be strictly exact in the service of the church. And when you have this *intention to please God in all your actions, as the happiest and best thing in the world,* you will find in you as great an aversion to anything that is vain and impertinent in common life, whether at business or pleasure, as you now have to any thing that is profane. You will be as fearful of living in any foolish way, either of spending your time, or your money, or indulging in any sinful desire or temper, as you now are fearful of neglecting the public worship of God."

Should the seeker of sanctification at any time fail of this intention, or of this resolution, let him not yield to discouragement, let him not think that it is impossible for him to obtain,— that God will hear his prayer no more: but rather let him imitate the child that is beginning to walk, who in coming to its parent, trips and falls, and crying, gets up and runs, till it falls again, and so continues to fall and to run, till finally it reaches its parent. Thus should the person do that would seek full sanctification. Should he meet with outward opposition and persecution; or inward temptation and tribulation: should his views and feelings with respect to his own state change: should he even appear to himself more stupid, more wretched and helpless than ever, this should not discourage him or weaken his resolution. Though he may be ignorant of it, the work of sanctification is actually advancing so long as he keeps his resolution, or has strength to renew it when impaired. The oppositions and trials he meets with shall all be overruled for his good, and shall hasten the accomplishment of the work. He will in this way probably be brought to feel his own weakness more and more, till he can cast himself wholly on the strength of Christ, which shall be made perfect through his weakness.

4. And this must be a resolution to seek holiness, not at the hour of death, not some time or other, not at a future period, but *now* at the *present time*. A resolution that is

not carried into effect dies, and comes to nothing. This would be to conduct like thousands who feel their need of religion, and promise God that they will repent hereafter; but when the set time comes they feel no more disposition to repent than they did before: and thus putting the business off from time to time, they finally perish in their sins. When the prodigal son had resolved that he would arise and go to his father, it is added, "and he arose and came to his father." We must do likewise. — When the resolution is fully formed, that you will seek holiness, immediately set your face against all sin, even *all* the corruptions of your heart, confessing and bewailing them, and begging God for Christ's sake to take them all away and fill you with righteousness.

You may afterwards note this time more particularly. In order to strengthen your resolution, I would advise you to make a memorandum of it, and the time when formed, and entered upon, naming the day of the month and the hour of the day; and regard it as a covenant never to be broken or violated.

We may farther observe that God does not require us to be holy when we come to die, or at some indefinite time, or at a future period, but *now*. The law of God is not like the laws framed by men for the regulation of commerce, and which in some cases do not take place till a certain day: but it binds us at all times, from the beginning to the end of our life.

To day, the present time, is the voice both of the law and of the gospel; and every argument which can make it our duty and privilege to be holy at any time, makes it our duty and privilege to be so *now*. It is our duty and privilege *now* to have hearts perfectly cleansed from sin and filled with love. It was this consideration that drew from the apostle that earnest and affectionate expostulation in Rom. xii, 1, "I beseech you, therefore, brethren, by the mercies of God, that ye present your bodies a *liv-*

ing sacrifice, holy, acceptable unto God, which is your *reasonable* service."

But above all things, let it be observed that we are not to expect holiness by way of infusion, as water is poured into a vessel; but rather it is *wrought in us* by the power of the Spirit of God, on condition of our seeking and striving for it: How absurd and dangerous, therefore, would it be for us to put off the perfection of holiness till death, or till old age, or till a sick day, or a future period; when not only the time will be shorter and more uncertain, but all our difficulties will be increased many fold. Our bodily faculties will become impaired by age and disease, if we are not cut off by sudden death; and shall we put off a work of so much importance as the *perfecting of holiness in the fear of God,* to a time when we cannot promise ourselves one advantage that we do now enjoy, but when our trials and difficulties may, and probably will, be many times greater than they are at present. [sic] Besides, the work itself will become more difficult for being neglected. The sins of our hearts are like the weeds in our gardens, which are the more difficult to be destroyed as they multiply and take root.

This observation is corroborated by matter of fact. Those who come to their work with resolution, and especially in the first part of the Christian life, soon obtain complete deliverance from sin, and are made perfect in love; while those who have passed a long time in a justified state, without attempting to perfect holiness, acquire such habits of reasoning, doubting, distrusting, wanderings of heart and thought, that it becomes exceedingly hard, not to say impossible, for them to overcome.

The distance from justification to sanctification is not great, and is soon passed over, if we be obedient to our spiritual guide, and do not fall into idolatry, nor turn back in our hearts to spiritual Egypt. The children of Israel came to the borders of Canaan within a year and a half from their leaving Egypt, notwithstanding their frequent stoppings, and long stay at Mount Sinai, and the slow movement at all times of so large a multitude. But now they seem to have forgotten the wonders they had seen in the land of Ham, and the miracles which had attended their march through the wilderness, and they became faint hearted and fearful, and their unbelief suggested the necessity of sending spies; Deut. i, 22; they were not satisfied with God's promise, but would see for themselves. God hearkened to them in this thing, and ordered Moses to send men to search out the land. But those who could not trust the Lord were easily discouraged by the difficulties which lay in their way. On their return, the spies report: "We came unto the land whither thou sentest us, and surely it floweth with milk and honey; and this is the fruit of it. Nevertheless the people be strong that dwell in the land, and the cities are walled, and very great: and moreover we saw the children of *Anak* there.— We be not able to go up against the people; for they are stronger than we.— And all the congregation lifted up their voices, and cried saying, Would God we had died in the land of Egypt, or would God we had died in the wilderness. And they said one to another, Let us make a captain, and let us return into Egypt." In consequence of their murmurings, and their rebellion, God was displeased and ordered them to turn again to the wilderness where they were doomed to wander *forty years*. This was not in the original design of God concerning them. Had they been obedient to his command, they might have been in the possession of the promised land forty years sooner.

 Thus it is with many Christians: they are brought from the bondage of sin and Satan, and like the Israelites when they had passed the Red sea, record their deliverance in a song of praise to their Redeemer. While they are obedient they are sustained by bread from heaven, and their enemies are scattered before them. They follow their leader till they come to the very borders of perfect love; and when he would lead them on to the charge upon their inbred sin,— when he requires them to make the grand assault to dislodge the enemy from his strong hold in their hearts,— they become cowards, and give back. Forgetting, as it were, all the miracles of grace which have been wrought for them, they distrust their leader, the Captain of their salvation, and begin to talk of the number, the gigantic size and strength of the corruptions of their hearts. They admit that entire sanctification is a good land, and the fruit of it delicious to the taste; but then they are not able to go up and possess it. They must wait till death, for the destruction of all their inbred corruptions; thus forgetting the command utterly to destroy them,— Deut. vii, 2.

Here some break out into loud murmuring and disputing, and in their hearts turn back to spiritual Egypt, preferring their former bondage to the fatigue and danger attendant on their warfare and complete conquest of the land of promise. Their love soon grows cold, they are entangled again in the yoke of bondage, and after wandering about a long time in the wilderness, parched with drought, and wasted with hunger, they miserably perish. Some absurdly make a league with inbred sin, as the Israelites did with the *Gibeonites,* to spare its life as long as they live; while others, unwilling to make the needful sacrifice, look upon the world and the things that are in it, much as *Achan* did when he saw a "goodly Babylonish garment, and two hundred shekels of silver, and a wedge of gold of fifty shekels weight," and coveting the spoil, take it and hide it away in their hearts.

But the few Calebs or Joshuas who "have another spirit in them, and who fully follow the Lord," are determined neither to make a parley or hold a truce nor give quarters to their enemies; but encouraging themselves in the Lord, are bold to say, "We are well able to go up against them and overcome." And according to their faith it is done unto them. In vain does Jordan roll its current athwart their way — in vain does *Jericho* oppose its strong and towering walls. The priests of the Lord, bearing the ark of the covenant, the Word of God, and going before them, the waters of Jordan are cut off to make them a passage, and the greatest difficulties are overcome without injury. Jericho, the polluted heart, is besieged, surrounded, and straitly shut up. So closely is it watched that "none go out, and none come in." Prayer is offered to God day and night, and the "Spirit maketh intercession with groanings that cannot be uttered." Faith has taken hold on the divine promise, and trusts in the power of God to effect the work. They are more and more conscious that the work is the Lord's and that all they can do is no more than the mere sound of rams' horns: yet they continue to cry to the Lord for help; and he says, "Thy name shall be called Israel: for as a prince hast thou power with God, and hast prevailed." In that moment leave is given to shout; while, before victorious faith every difficulty subsides like the falling walls of Jericho, and the enemy is put to the sword; inbred sin is all destroyed, and "grace reigns unto eternal life." The conquest is complete, and he enjoys that rest on earth, which God has provided for his people.

Why should we not go up at once, and possess this goodly land that flows with milk and honey? Why should we not go on from the commencement to the perfection of the work of grace? The course is short, and the difficulties comparatively few, when we first experience the kingdom of God set up in our hearts. We cannot be too soon, nor too much in earnest about this business. — "Wherefore, leaving the principles of the doctrine of Christ, let us go on to perfection."

5. Being convinced of the importance of complete sanctification, and being resolved to seek it, and to set about it now, remember you are to receive it by faith. He that cometh unto God, must believe that He is the rewarder of them that seek sanctification, or the forgiveness of sin. "The just shall live by faith." By faith we stand— by faith we walk— by faith we are saved. Faith worketh by love, and is therefore of the most immediate use to purify the soul. "Hence it is, that Christ, the prophets and the apostles, so strongly insist upon *faith;* assuring us that if we will 'not believe,' we shall not be established,— and that if we will 'believe, we shall see the glory of God.'

"They tell us, that Christ gave himself for the church, that he might sanctify and cleanse it 'by the word,'— that he might present it to himself a glorious church, not having spot or wrinkle, or any such thing, but that it should be holy and without blemish. Now, if believers are to be cleansed and made without blemish *by the word,* (which testifies of the all-atoning blood, and the love of the Spirit) it is evident they are to be sanctified *by faith;* for *faith* or *believing* has as necessary a reference to the *word,* as *eating* has to *food.*"

And the Scriptures abundantly testify that "they who believe enter into rest;" that a promise being left us of entering in, we should take care not to fall short of it *through unbelief;* that we are "filled with *all* joy and *peace* in *believing;* and that Christ is able to *save to the uttermost* them that believe in him." For "God, who knoweth the hearts" (of the penitent believers who hunger and thirst after righteousness) "bears them witness, giving them the Holy Ghost, *purifying their hearts by faith;*" for, says Jesus, they are "*sanctified* by *faith* that is in me."

Indeed the whole work of our salvation is carried on through *faith;* because salvation is the gift of God, and *faith* the *receiver* of that gift. Faith is every where spoken of as the medium through which the blessings of the gospel come to us— they are *by* faith, *through* faith, &c.

But what is that faith whereby we are *sanctified,* saved from sin, and perfected in love? I cannot so well answer this question as in Mr. Wesley's words, in his sermon called "The Scripture way of salvation." This faith "is a Divine evidence and conviction, 1. That God hath promised this sanctification in the Holy Scriptures. Till we are thoroughly satisfied of this, there is no moving one step farther. And one would imagine there needed not one word more to satisfy a reasonable man of this, than the ancient promise, 'Then will I circumcise thy heart, and the heart of thy seed, to love the Lord thy God with all thy heart, and with all thy soul, and with all thy mind!' How clearly does this express the being perfected in love? How imply the being saved from all sin? For as long as love takes up the whole heart, what room is there for sin therein?

2. "It is a Divine evidence and conviction that what God hath promised he is *able* to perform. Admitting therefore that with men it is impossible to bring a clean thing out of an unclean, to purify the heart from all sin, and to fill it with all holiness; yet this creates no difficulty in the case, seeing 'with God all things are possible.' And surely no one ever imagined it was possible to any power less than that of the Almighty! But if God speaks, it shall be done. God saith, 'Let there be light,' and there is light.

3. "It is a Divine evidence and conviction that he is able and *willing* to do it *now.* And why not? Is not a moment to him the same as a thousand years? He cannot want more time to accomplish whatever is his will. And he cannot want or stay for any more *worthiness* or *fitness* in the persons he is pleased to honour. We may therefore boldly say, at any point of time, 'now is the day of salvation.' 'To day if ye will hear his voice, harden not your hearts.' 'Behold! all things are *now* ready, come unto the marriage!'

4. "To this confidence that God is both able and willing to sanctify us *now,* there needs to be added one thing more, a divine evidence and conviction that *he doeth it.*" Mr. Wesley says, "believe that he *doeth it.*" But this is a different thing from believing that he *hath accomplished* it. Some have supposed that to obtain the evidence of sanctification, you must believe the work accomplished, and profess it. But this is not the thing intended. You cannot rightly believe the work accomplished before the evidence is produced in your soul. But you may believe that he *doeth it,* that is, that he is *doing* it, that he has begun, is carrying on, and is willing and ready on his part, *now* to accomplish it. If you believe this, and at the same time keep in view that your complete sanctification is contained in the gospel offer and promise, you will be enabled to embrace it. And when you have done so, you shall know that you have it in possession. The object of your faith is not so properly something to be done, as something that already exists. And what is that which already exists, but the provision made for your entire sanctification, the offer and promise of this in the gospel, the beginning of the work in your soul, the continued agency of the Holy Ghost in exciting your desires for it, and prompting and assisting your efforts to lay hold on it? When you believe this with a full reliance, the blessing is yours. "In that hour it is done. God says to the inmost soul, 'according to thy faith be it unto thee!' Then the soul is pure from every spot of sin; 'it is clean from all unrighteousness.' The believer then experiences the deep meaning of those solemn words, 'If we walk in the light as he is in the light, we have fellowship one with another, and the blood of Jesus Christ, his Son, cleanseth us from all sin.'"

But does God work this great work in the soul gradually, or instantaneously? "Perhaps," says Mr. Wesley, "it may be gradually wrought in some; I mean, in this sense, they do not advert to the particular moment wherein sin ceases to be. It is infinitely desirable, were it the will of God, that it should be done instantaneously; that the Lord should destroy sin 'by the breath of his mouth,' in a moment, in the twinkling of an eye. And so he generally does; a plain fact, of which there is evidence enough to satisfy any unprejudiced person. *Thou,* therefore, look for it every moment. Look for it in the way above described. There is no danger: you can be no worse, if you are no better, for that expectation. But you shall not be disappointed of your hope: it will come, and will not tarry. Look for it then every day, every hour, every moment. Why not this hour, this moment? Certainly you may look for it *now,* if you believe it is by faith. And by this token you may surely know whether you seek it by faith or by works. If by works, you want something to be done *first, before* you are sanctified. You think, 'I must first *be* or *do* thus or thus.' Then you are seeking it by works unto this day. If you seek it by faith, you may expect it *as you are:* then expect it *now.* It is of importance to observe that there is an inseparable connexion between these three points, expect it by *faith,* expect it *as you are,* and expect it *now.* To deny one of them is to deny them all. To allow one is to allow them all. Do *you* believe we are sanctified by faith? Be true then to your principle, and look for this blessing just as you are, neither better nor worse; as a poor sinner that has nothing to pay, nothing to plead but the merits of Christ. And if you look for it as you are, then expect it *now.* Stay for nothing: why should you? Christ is ready, and he is all you want. He is waiting for you: he is at the door! Let your inmost soul cry out,

'Come in, come in, thou heavenly guest!
  Nor hence again remove;
Settle and fix my wav'ring breast
  With all thy weight of love.'"

But here it will be asked whether something beside faith is not necessary? Whether repentance and good works, as well as faith, are not indispensable conditions of sanctification?

To this it may be replied: it is allowed that repentance, or a conviction of the remaining corruptions of our hearts, and the fruits of that repentance, are necessary to full sanctification; "yet," says Mr. Wesley, "they are not necessary either in the *same sense* with faith, or in the *same degree:* not in the same degree; for these fruits are necessary *conditionally,* if there be time and opportunity for them; otherwise, a man may be sanctified without them. But he cannot be *sanctified* without faith. Likewise let a man have ever so much of this repentance, or ever so many good works, yet all this does not avail: he is not *sanctified* till he believes. But the moment he believes, with or without these fruits, yea, with more or less of this repentance, he is *sanctified.* Not in the *same sense,* for this repentance and these fruits are only *remotely* necessary; necessary in order to the continuance of his faith, as well as the increase of it; whereas faith is *immediately* and *directly* necessary to sanctification. It remains that faith is the only condition which is immediately necessary to sanctification."

6. I have said that repentance, and the fruits meet for repentance, are necessary, "if there be time and opportunity for them;" that is, if you are not so happy as to obtain this great salvation now, you must wait for it in the use of all the means of grace, striving continually against all sin, and looking every moment for Christ to come and take full possession of your heart. And remember, you are not to suppose that he cannot cleanse you while you are so unclean, or that he cannot empty you of sin and fill you with righteousness in a moment. A day, an hour, a moment, with him is as good as a thousand years to

sanctify your soul. Expect the blessing, therefore, every time you ask for it. And hath he not said, "Ask, and it shall be given unto you; seek, and ye shall find; knock, and it shall be opened unto you." Let your soul continually be going out after the Lord: look for him when you join with the congregation in prayer: look for him when you more privately join with your brethren in prayer. Here you may use the utmost freedom. Let your brethren know the particulars of your case,— ask their prayers,— join with them, and lift up one united cry to him who is able to save. If you do not find him here, look for him in your closet. And remember, that Jacob wrestled and prevailed, being alone. Christ was transfigured while he prayed alone, the disciples being asleep. And many have found this blessing alone, after wrestling till midnight, or till the cock's crowing, or till the breaking of the day. And when you come before God to ask this blessing, see that you do not ask doubtingly or fearingly, as though you had no right to expect so great a blessing; but rather "come boldly to the throne of grace, that you may obtain mercy, and find grace to help in time of need." You undoubtedly have a right, you have a claim in the name of Christ. The blessing you seek was purchased for you by Christ when he made his soul an offering for sin; and it is now sincerely and freely *offered* to you in the gospel. The *offer* constitutes a ground of claim, far better than though you could claim it as a debt due to you. Behold, the Saviour stands, and stretching out his hands to you, says, "Hitherto ye have asked nothing (comparatively) in my name: ask and receive, that your joy may be full. When ye pray, believe that ye receive the things ye ask for, and ye shall have them." —*Believe that ye receive them,* believe that ye receive full sanctification in and with Christ, lay hold on it, claim it as your own, *and ye shall have it.* Say not that you are unworthy, that you are unfit. The blessed Saviour knows you *are* unworthy, but he means to make you worthy by sanctifying you for himself. Therefore, I say again, lay hold on the blessing, and it is yours: lay hold on him who of God is made unto you *sanctification,* as well as righteousness and redemption. Press through the crowd of temptations, fears, and oppositions, from within and without, and touch if it be but the hem of the Saviour's garment; for the slightest touch of faith will bring sanctifying virtue out of him, to your longing, fainting soul.

To conclude this subject:— When a soul is thoroughly convinced of the importance of sanctification, and comes and throws himself at the feet of Christ, making all the effort in his power to receive him as his complete Saviour, let him not feel discouraged if he should not be immediately met by Christ, according to his wishes. Let him not think his efforts are disregarded by him whom he seeks. Though he tarry, wait for him, because he will surely come, and will not tarry. *Rest in the Lord, and wait patiently for him.* "I waited patiently for the Lord," says the psalmist, "and he inclined unto me, and heard my cry." You must wait *for* him, in the way of waiting *upon* him. Wait in the way of resisting every temptation of the devil, every sinful inclination of your heart; wait upon him in the use of all the means of grace, and crying incessantly to him for help, and you shall not cry in vain. "The Lord whom ye seek shall suddenly come to his temple, even the Messenger of the covenant whom ye delight in: behold he shall come, saith the Lord of hosts." Many have sought without obtaining an immediate answer, as Jacob, and Job, and David, and the Syrophenician woman. God may delay a little to bestow this blessing upon you, for reasons worthy of himself. You may not be ready to receive it, though you think you are. God may delay a little, to excite a greater earnestness in your soul for it, or to teach you in some measure the value of it before you receive it, that you may hold it fast when you have obtained it. But as he did not long delay in the cases referred to above, so neither will he in yours. For he has not *said to the seed of Jacob, Seek ye me in vain.*

7. Having given these rules for the direction of those who would seek the sanctification of their souls, it may not be amiss to point out a little more clearly that state of mind, and those exercises, which, in a greater or less degree, precede and accompany the attainment of that great blessing.

As it is not everyone who says, "Lord, Lord, that shall enter into the kingdom of heaven," so it is not everyone who believes the doctrine, and allows that sanctification is a good thing, that shall enjoy that blessing; but he, and he only, who is willing to make every sacrifice to obtain it. As there are many who assent to the truth of the doctrines of justification and regeneration, without ever coming to the knowledge of true religion; so there are many who believe the doctrine of sanctification, without knowing what it is by experience.

Generally, some time after justification, there is a conviction wrought in the soul of the necessity of a deeper work of grace. There is, at this time, a discovery of much remaining corruption of nature, and such evils as were thought to be wholly destroyed, or to have no existence. This is an important period in the life of a Christian. He now needs the best instruction, and the tenderest dealing; otherwise he is liable on one hand to conclude he was never converted, or on the other to imagine he must always remain in his present condition, and suffer the evils he feels as long as he lives. If he be rightly taught he will guard against both these errors; and while he holds fast his confidence in his free justification, he will go on and seek to be cleansed from all the remaining pollutions of his nature. Under this view his conviction becomes clearer, and he is led to view a depth and an extent of depravity which he had never before seen. In proportion as his views become clearer, and he abhors himself on account of the sin of his nature, he desires an inward and perfect conformity to the image of God, which consists in righteousness and true holiness. Through various reasonings and temptations, the progress of the work is generally slow; but though it be retarded, it is not altogether hindered. He sees and feels that he ought to love God with all his heart and his neighbour as himself. He *feels* that the law of God requireth truth in the inward parts, and that it is a discerner of the thoughts and intents of the heart. This conviction often diminishes the lustre of his past experience, as the light of a candle is nearly lost in the transcendant [sic] rays of the sun; but this so far from discouraging him, only serves to make him cry the more earnestly that God would create in him a clean heart, and renew a right spirit within him.

Thus cherishing his conviction, his light still increases, his views of his state become more painful, and his inmost soul cries out for God, for the living God, and refuses to be comforted, till God shall appear for him, and

> "Speak the second time, be clean,
> Take away the inward sin;
> Every stumblingblock remove,
> Fill his heart with perfect love."

His heart being fixed, the trials he meets with, whether from within or without, do not hinder him, but rather serve to inflame his desires after God, and a full restoration to his image. The glories of the world have faded in his sight, a sickly hue is cast upon all sublunary things; and nothing but the possession of the Supreme God can satisfy the longing desire of his soul. He is sick of love, love to the crucified, and ready to cry out at every breath, "Set me as a seal upon thy heart; as a seal upon thy arm;

for love is strong as death; jealousy is cruel as the grave; the coals thereof are coals of fire which hath a most vehement flame." And the following prayer may, perhaps, suit his occasion: —

> Oh, Almighty and most merciful God! permit a penitent sinner to come into thy presence, and make supplication unto thee. Thou, oh Lord, art holy, and highly exalted; but I am unworthy, and exceedingly vile. I am a fallen creature, and my soul is defiled within me. Thou requirest truth in the inward parts, but I am filled with the corruption of my nature. Behold, I was conceived in sin, and shapen in iniquity; and like the wild ass's colt, I have been prone to go astray from the beginning of my days. My heart departed from thee, and my desires and affections became fixed on many objects; my will grew perverse and stubborn; my understanding was darkened; and from the head even unto the foot there is no soundness in me, but I am full of wounds, bruises, and putrefying sores. My whole head is sick, and my whole heart faint. I am altogether as an unclean thing.
>
> I have this farther addition to my native depravity, that when thou didst put into my hands the means of purifying myself from all filthiness of flesh and spirit, I did not use them for this purpose. Thou hast opened a fountain for sin and uncleanness; but I have not washed away my sin. I have been indifferent to my greatest interests. I have been lukewarm when I ought to have been filled with holy resolution and zeal. While my conduct has been marked with the greatest ingratitude and folly, in delaying my perfect cleansing, the evil propensities of my nature have been striking deeper root, and entrenching themselves in my heart. My heart which ought to have been opened to thee as thy temple, has remained the hold of every unclean and hateful bird. This rendered

my efforts to serve thee feeble and ineffectual, consumed the comforts of thy grace, and brought languor and heartlessness into my devotions. And that I have not wholly apostatized from thee is owing to thy tender mercy, and not to any virtue of my own.

And now, oh Lord, what shall I say unto thee! For I am exceedingly filled with shame and trouble. My wounds stink and are corrupt, because of my foolishness. I am troubled, I am bowed down greatly: I go mourning all the day long. For my loins are filled with a loathsome disease, and there is no soundness in my flesh. Oh Lord, all my desire is unto thee, and my groaning is not hid from thee. My heart panteth, my strength faileth me: as for the light which once shone within, and comforted me, it no longer satisfies me. But since thou hast given me this discovery of the depth of my depravity, I cannot rest till it be removed, and I am fully restored to thine image. Since thou hast given me to see thy holiness, I abhor myself, and repent in dust and ashes.

Unto thee, O Lord, do I lift up my soul, for my help can only come from thee. Remember, oh Lord, thy tender mercies, and thy loving kindnesses, for they have been ever of old. Oh, keep my soul and deliver me, for I put my trust in thee. Behold, thou desirest truth in the inward parts; and in the hidden parts thou shalt make me to know wisdom. Purge me, and I shall be clean; wash me, and I shall be whiter than snow. Create in me a clean heart, oh God, and renew a right spirit within me. Give unto me the joys of thy great salvation, and uphold me with thy free Spirit.

And hast not thou promised, oh my God, that thou wilt do all this for them who call upon thee? Hast thou not engaged to sprinkle clean water upon them and cleanse them from all their idols, and from all their filthiness? And is it not written that if they confess their sins, thou wilt forgive them, and cleanse them from all unrighteousness? I know it is thy word, and I cast myself upon it. I come to thee oh Lord my God, not in my own name, not mentioning my own righteousness, which is as filthy rags, but in the name of Jesus Christ, thy well beloved Son, and plead his merits for my cleansing and healing. Behold, oh God, my shield; and look upon the face of thine anointed. Didst thou not give him that he might become my wisdom, righteousness, *sanctification,* and redemption? I know thou didst; and I would receive him now as my sanctification and my all. I would receive him in all his offices, that I might partake of all his benefits. Let him be so revealed and formed within me, that I may say, with thy servant Paul, I am crucified with Christ, nevertheless I live; yet not I, but Christ liveth in me, and the life I now live, I live by faith in the Son of God, who loved me and gave himself for me. Thou seest, Lord, that I would be thine, that I would love thee with all my heart, soul, mind, and strength, and that I would glorify thee in my body and spirit, which are thine. And this is thy will also—I know it is: thou hast commanded it. Thou hast promised to circumcise my heart that I may thus love and glorify thee. And thou art able to save to the uttermost all that come unto thee. Thy hand is not shortened that it cannot save; neither is thine ear heavy, that it cannot hear. And now, oh Lord, I give myself up to thee; I resign my own will, and embrace thine in all things. I henceforth leave it with thee to appoint me the service thou pleasest, and to choose whatever trials thou seest will be for my good. I take thee, FATHER, SON, and HOLY SPIRIT, for my portion and my all. And when thou shalt have perfected me, and served thyself of me in this world, receive me to thyself through Jesus Christ my Lord. Amen.

Chapter IV.
The Most Common Difficulties in the Way of Seeking Christian Perfection Considered and Removed.

IT IS NECESSARY IN every piece of work, to begin right; and especially in seeking so great a blessing as that of sanctification. But many who are convinced of the need of that blessing, know not how to begin the work; or if they begin, they soon meet with difficulties which discourage them, and cause them to stop. The principal difficulties which I have met with, in conversing with those whose minds were exercised about sanctification, I propose here to state, and briefly consider; that the sincere may see their way clear before them, and be enabled to go on to perfection.

1. Many stumble at the very threshold, for want, as they suppose, of the necessary conviction to begin and proceed in the work.

There is often an error committed here. It is not necessary that all should have the same degree of conviction, in order to seek either justification or sanctification. Many who have had a degree of conviction, have delayed setting about the work in both cases, because they supposed their convictions were not deep enough. They have prayed for conviction, as though they expected it immediately from heaven; and because they could not obtain it in this way, they have been perplexed, and nearly driven into despair. At the same time I acknowledge, that without conviction nothing can be done. But conviction is a different thing from what many suppose. Its seat is not in the imagination, but in the conscience; and it consists not so much in terror, as in a just view of the nature of sin. This conviction is produced by the divine law applied to our actions, or to the dispositions and propensities of our nature. Conviction in those who have been born of the Spirit, is a discovery of the remaining corruptions of their nature, which are to be done away by sanctification.

The present inquiry is, how much of this conviction is necessary to enable one to seek complete sanctification? And I suppose that, to believe in the doctrine of sanctification, and at the same time to know that he has not experienced it, is all that is *necessary* in order to commence the work. More may be necessary afterwards, and God will not fail to give it as it is necessary. He gives at first what is necessary to commence with: and why should anyone expect more, till he has used what he already has? It is with this, as it is with every other talent, it is increased by being used.

Perhaps your conviction at present is nothing more than a rational persuasion, that you need a deeper work—an entire renovation of nature. Your heart is not pained, neither is your conscience distressed, with your situation. But you believe it is your duty to be sanctified wholly. Go on, then, and seek sanctification; and be not troubled about the degree of conviction you have, or have not. God will take care of that. Conviction will come in due time. You are to aim at pleasing God in every thought, word, and action. It is your duty to love God with all your heart, and to glorify him in your body and spirit, which are his. You must resolutely set about this, and cry to God for grace to enable you to do so. You must resign your will in all things. You must present yourself unto God as one alive from the dead. This is your duty: you must aim at this. And while you are striving to exercise faith, love, patience, meekness, humility, &c, you will feel all the remaining sin of your nature stirred up to make opposition. And when you feel it, confess it. Lament it as you are able. Bring it before the Lord, and cry to him to slay it and take it away, that you may have nothing within to oppose your loving and serving God with all your heart.

If a man who is sailing with the stream would feel the strength and opposition of it, he must turn about, and stem the current: and if you would feel the strength and opposition of your evil propensities, and sinful tempers and passions, you must turn from them, and oppose them all, by endeavouring to practice the opposite virtues; and you will be sure to feel their utmost strength, or rather, all that is necessary.

This, however, depends in a great measure on the clearness of your views of sanctification, of the nature and extent of Christian perfection. Some people, because they have not clear views of these, have perplexed and indistinct impressions of their state, both before and after sanctification. If, therefore, he who seeks after sanctification would succeed, let him labour after a clear and distinct understanding of his object. And as all our knowledge upon this subject is derived from the Scriptures, he must search these with diligence and prayer, especially the Epistle of St. John, where this great blessing is most fully and clearly described. He may also derive much assistance from well-written treatises upon the subject, and by conversation with those who have attained to that state. But in no stage of the work should the seeker of sanctification feel discouragement because his conviction is not so deep as he thinks it should be; but rather let him seek for clear ideas upon the subject of gospel perfection, and then go on to perfect holiness in the fear of God; leaving the degree of conviction, and every other circumstance of the work, to him who is infinitely wise and merciful. In this way, he cannot fail of success. But if he undertakes to lay out the work for God, to appoint him the time and manner of his working, he will most assuredly be disappointed. As this is particularly the work of grace, and as God will have all the honour of man's salvation, so he *will bring the blind by a way they have not known.*

2. While some professedly halt for want of conviction, others have so much, and see so much sin in themselves, that they are quite discouraged.

It is generally the case with those who are born of God, that they rejoice for a while, with joy unspeakable and full of glory. They feel a great change wrought in them — are wholly taken up with the contemplation of that free, abundant grace which has been bestowed upon them. During this favoured season, the motions of sin are suspended, and the remaining corruptions of their hearts hid from their sight, and nothing is more natural than to conclude that there is no sin remaining in them, because they feel none. But God will not suffer them to remain under this mistake long. He will show them the comparative weakness of all their graces, and the remaining depravity of their nature. Accordingly, when trials come, their faith, and peace, and love, are put to the test; and though not destroyed, they are found to be weak. On the other hand, much unbelief, hardness of heart, self will, anger, impatience, and a train of evils, remain in the heart, and cause pain, inexpressible pain, though they have the victory over them. Here they are thrown into perplexity. Their experience of God's grace appears much less than it did, even if they hold fast their confidence; and those evil propensities which they thought were entirely destroyed, are yet alive in great abundance and strength within them. And the inference they draw is this, that it is impossible for them to obtain full sanctification.

But let such understand, that if they have not knowingly sinned, nor yielded to temptation, the discovery of inbred sin is so far from being a proof that they are less in the favour of God than they before thought, that it is an additional blessing, and just cause of gratitude and encouragement. God has given them this discovery not in wrath, but love, not as an indication that they are doomed to carry it as long as they live in the body; but that they may repent of it, and wash it away in the *fountain opened for sin and uncleanness.*

And why should any discouragement be indulged from a discovery of all the evils remaining in the heart? Is not Christ "able to save to the uttermost all them that come unto God by him?" And though all the earth should be moved against you, and though the devil should come with his most subtle, powerful temptations, be not discouraged in the least. And even if you do not soon obtain deliverance, but your prospects become more dark, and you feel more and more wretched, still persevere in calling upon the strong for help. "His hand is not shortened that it cannot save; neither is his ear heavy, that it cannot hear." Remember it is written, "If we confess our sins, he is faithful and just, to forgive us our sins, and to cleanse us from all unrighteousness." *God will not leave nor forsake you;* but having given his own Son for you while you were enemies; how much more will he, in and with his Son, freely give you all things, and this above all, deliverance from sin!

3. It was said above, that at the time of the discovery of this inbred sin, the experience of God's grace appears much less than before, even if they hold fast their confidence. But how frequently is their confidence shaken. How often do they cast it away, and conclude they were never born of God, and have miserably deceived themselves. If they hold their confidence for a time, and resolve not to rest in their present state, but seek a clean heart, and the fulness of love, yet they are apt to give it up afterwards. For it is commonly the case that such find so much sin remaining in them, and the corruptions of their hearts are so chafed and irritated, by being restrained and opposed, that they do not perceive the evidence of the grace they have received. And to this, that what they lack is so much greater than what they have received, that the evidence of the latter is greatly obscured.

But this is an error, and should be carefully guarded against. It is no evidence that one is not justified and born of God, because he finds much sin remaining. God accepted and pardoned him when he was altogether ungodly, and will he cast him off now, because sin remaineth in him? Observe, we are not now speaking of one who has drawn back from the Lord, who has yielded himself up to the government of his carnal desires and passions; but of him who has a discovery of his remaining sin. He has no more sin now, but far less, than when God accepted him for Christ's sake. All the difference lies in a different view of himself. When God justified and adopted him freely, he saw it, and rejoiced in that grace; there was at that time as much sin remaining in him as he now discovers, and perhaps more; but he knew it not, although his God knew it; and surely God will not take his loving kindness from him for a cause which existed when he

IV. THE MOST COMMON DIFFICULTIES IN THE WAY OF SEEKING CONSIDERED AND REMOVED | 109

bestowed it. His state is certainly not the worse, for his having more knowledge of himself than he then had. God accepted him at first, not for his own sake, for he was altogether a sinner, and unworthy; but for the alone sake of Jesus Christ. And as he accepted him at first for Christ's sake, so he will continue to accept him and treat him as a beloved child, notwithstanding all the remaining sin of his nature. Only let him not give place to unbelief. Let him "not cast away his confidence, which has great recompense of reward."

Indeed, if he cast away his confidence, the work is, for the present at least, at a stand; and he may backslide, make shipwreck of the faith, and lose all that he has hitherto wrought. A loving confidence in the mercy of God is of the utmost importance to the increase of the work of grace upon the heart. While the Christian holds fast this, sin cannot *"reign over him,"* though it may *"remain in him,"* and he may feel the inward motions of it more painful than coals of fire. And if it appear a hazardous presumption to believe himself a child of God while so much sin remains in him; yet let him be assured that it is unbelief and temptation which so represent it; and that he will be none the better, but far worse for giving up his confidence, and withdrawing his trust in the mercy of God. In that case he will hinder the work of God in his soul, and give sin the dominion over him; which, otherwise, is chained and under his feet. Besides, were his state what he is tempted to think it is, what could he do for himself? How could he remedy it? How, but by going and throwing himself on the mercy of God in Christ? This is the only way to become or remain the children of God. The sinner is justified by faith; and by faith he stands in that grace, and by faith he walks, and by faith he lives, and by faith he is saved, and without faith it is impossible to please God. If he hold fast his confidence, and endure the painful sight of himself, confessing his corruption, and pleading the merits of Christ, he shall soon feel a powerful application of the atoning blood, to cleanse him from all filthiness of the flesh and of the spirit, and to renew him in the spirit and temper of his mind. It is possible that they *may* be pardoned and cleansed from all filthiness of flesh and spirit in the same moment. There is nothing impossible with God in this.

Mr. Wesley admits that if any have from the time of their justification "*total resignation* to the will of God, without any mixture of self will; *gentleness*, without any touch of anger the moment they are provoked; *love* to God, without the least love to the creature, but in and for God, excluding *all* pride; love to man, excluding *all* envy, *all* jealousy, and rash judging; *meekness*, keeping the whole soul inviolably calm; and *temperance* in all things;" that "they are sanctified, saved from sin in that moment: and they need never lose what God has given them, nor feel sin anymore." But this is far from being God's usual method of working. "God usually gives time," says the author last quoted, "for men to receive light, to grow in grace, to do and suffer his will, before they are either justified or sanctified."

"Sometimes," says the venerable Wesley, again, "he cuts his work short. He does the work of many years in a few weeks: perhaps in a week, a day, or an hour. He justifies, or sanctifies, both those who have done or suffered nothing, and who have not had time for a gradual growth, either in light or grace. And 'may he not do what he will with his own? Is thine eye evil because he is good?'"

We must not make that necessary to our justification or sanctification which God has not made necessary; and as he has revealed no rules, as to the time and manner of his operations, we must prescribe none. "He will bring the blind by a way they have not known." He will work in a way to "hide pride from man." Therefore, whosoever thou art, that findest thy need of sanctification; go

IV. THE MOST COMMON DIFFICULTIES IN THE WAY OF SEEKING CONSIDERED AND REMOVED | 111

and fall down before thy God, and there confess thy ignorance, thy weakness, thy sinfulness, and utter helplessness. Claim nothing but the salvation of thy soul; and that not for thine own wisdom or goodness, but for the alone merits of thy Saviour. And at whatever time thy God shows thee that thou needest to be sanctified, and wholly set apart for himself; do not reply to him, that this cannot be done for thee now: that thou art too sinful: but rather consider it as a token of his gracious willingness and readiness to save thee to the uttermost— to save thee *now*. Check thine own vain, carnal reasonings; silence all thy objections; and, resigning thy will entirely, commit thyself to his mercy. So shalt thou be saved from all thy uncleanness, and he shall have the praise.

5. Others object that they have not been justified long enough, to warrant the expectation of full sanctification. This objection is in substance answered in the foregoing remarks, but he [*sic*] will give it a more distinct consideration.

Those who meet with this objection, or rather temptation, do not mean that they ought not to love God with all their heart, that they ought not to be perfectly holy now; but either that the work of sanctification is a gradual work, and they can only grow up to it little by little; or that they have not, since their justification, sufficiently seen and lamented the corruptions of their hearts.

With respect to the first part of this objection, that sanctification is a gradual work, and they can only grow up to it little by little, it may be observed, that the work may be accomplished in one day, or one hour, and yet be a gradual or progressive work. A long time is not necessary in order to a gradual work of this kind. The gradations may be as follows: 1. Light is imparted to the soul. 2. Conviction fastens upon the conscience. 3. A desire springs up to be delivered from all sin. 4. He confesses, and prays for deliverance. 5. He is convinced that he cannot cleanse his own heart, and therefore he casts himself upon the mercy of his God for this. 6. The work is wrought in him. Now it is evident that these several actions may be performed in a short time.

It is equally evident that this work is instantaneous, that is, that there is a moment when it is *accomplished*. And it is only with respect to the accomplishment of it, that it can be called instantaneous: unless indeed we speak of the whole process in a figurative way, and call that instantaneous, which is performed in a very short time. This, it appears, some writers have done; but Mr. Wesley, whose views are always clear upon this subject, considers the work instantaneous with respect to the time when sin is all done away. "A man," says he, "may be dying for some time; yet he does not, properly speaking, *die*, till the instant the soul is separated from the body: and in that instant, he lives the life of eternity. In like manner, he may be *dying to sin*, for some time: yet he is not *dead to sin* until sin is separated from the soul. And in that instant he lives the full life of love. As the change undergone when the body dies, is of a different kind, and infinitely greater than any we had known before, yea such as till then it is impossible to conceive; so the change wrought when the soul dies to sin, is of a different kind, and infinitely greater than any before, and than any can conceive till he experiences it."

And we may add, that if the entire sanctification of our souls is a blessing bestowed by God and received by us, there must be an instant when it is given and received. And though we cannot always distinguish that moment from the moment which goes before, or from that which follows, yet we can have no doubt that it exists.

With respect to the other part of the objection, which relates to the time of seeing and lamenting the corruptions of nature, it has the appearance of seeking by works, and not by faith. At least those who make this objection

IV. THE MOST COMMON DIFFICULTIES IN THE WAY OF SEEKING CONSIDERED AND REMOVED | 113

are not clear in their views of the way in which that blessing is to be obtained.

Indeed, a person cannot lament too much the pollution of his nature; but he may place too much *dependance* [sic] on his lamentations. We must be sensible that our repentance merits neither justification, nor sanctification; and though it be a condition of both, yet, as a condition, it is necessary only as it brings us to Christ. When, therefore, a fallen child of man sees his naked and helpless condition, and feels a disposition to go to Christ for what he needs, he never need to fear that he shall be rejected because his repentance is not deep enough. And were he to spend the longest life in lamenting his sins, it would not atone for one transgression, nor wash out one stain from his polluted soul. In a gospel point of view he would be no nearer sanctification, than when he began the cause of penitence. He may as well, therefore, go now, and go just as he is, as to wait a longer time to lament his inbred corruptions.

"By this token," says Mr. Wesley, "you may surely know whether you seek it by faith or by works. If by works, you want something to be done, *first, before* you are sanctified. You think, I must *first* be, or do, thus or thus. Then you are seeking it by works unto this day. If you seek it by faith, you may expect it *as you are*. Then expect it *now*."

Thus you see there is no weight in the objection that you have not been justified long enough to expect sanctification. The voice of God to you is, "Be ye, therefore, perfect, even as your Father who is in heaven is perfect." And St. Paul says, "Leaving, therefore, the principles," the first rudiments, "of the doctrine of Christ, let us go on to perfection." He does not tell you that you have not been justified long enough to obey these commands, or to expect this great salvation. So far from that, that this is the most favourable time you will ever have. The longer you delay, the more, a great deal, will your difficulties increase. The evil propensities of your nature will increase their strength, and take deeper root. You will contract habits of reasoning and doubting, which you will find very difficult to conquer. Your mind will become dissipated, and your thoughts scattered. Temptation will gain the ascendancy over you in a thousand ways of which you do not conceive.

If you would prevent this increase of difficulties, begin immediately, and seek full sanctification, and never stop till you obtain it. If you are young in years, as well as in experience, your advantages are greater still. There is a flexibility of mind in *youth* which is of the utmost importance in religion. It renders you more susceptible of good impressions, and more readily takes a right direction, than the stiffness of age. We may observe at any time that a much larger proportion of youth experience religion, than of those in old age, or even in middle age; and it is a fact that a much larger proportion experience sanctification. Indeed it is rare that any of those who have lived a number of years in the common way of Christians, without aiming at perfection, attain to that exalted state of piety before death. And this shows the importance of beginning in early life, and in the early part of the Christian life, to perfect holiness, without which no man shall see the Lord.

There is another consideration which has great weight in it. Whoever would reach the highest attainments in religion, has a great work to do. Self must be denied and subdued. The will must be brought into perfect subjection to the will of God; in order to which, sacrifices must be made and privations endured. And there is a time when this work is comparatively easy, viz., in the first part of the Christian life, when the mind feels the importance, and acts under the influence of those objects and motives which have so lately been brought into operation with him. If he overrun the present favourable circumstances, he will not feel as willing to make sacrifices and deny himself; his conscience will become less tender, the fear and love of God will have less influence over him; those attachments and connexions which had been wounded, weakened, and suspended, in his religious experience, will revive; and it is a great wonder if he do not slide into those habits of thinking, conversing, and living, which prevail with the great body of fashionable Christians around him. Therefore, while his heart is warm with the love of God, and he burns with an ardent zeal for the glory of God, let him go on to perfection. This is peculiarly his time. He is now strong, and the comforts of the Holy Ghost are multiplied in him. He will do more in one day now than in a month when he is weakened in the way. He has been long enough justified to go on to perfection.

6. It is frequently the case that those who are exercised about sanctification, and believe in the doctrine, think it would be *presumption* for them to ask for it. They believe others may experience it, that many have experienced it; but it is not for them.

And how many sinners under conviction have the same thoughts? Viewing themselves as unworthy, it appears to them presumption to ask for what others, as unworthy as themselves, have sought and found. This is a temptation which very naturally occurs; but it is dissipated, and made to vanish by the declaration of the gospel. Jesus Christ commands us to be *perfect,* and promises to make us so. And can it be presumption in us to aim at what he commands? Can it be presumption in us to rely upon his promises, and claim them as true? Presumption consists not in receiving the commands and promises of Jesus Christ, but in rejecting them. If we were told in the gospel that perfection is not for all, then the plea of presumption would have plausibility; or if God gave us only according to our merits, it would be presumption in anyone to ask, not only for perfection but for the smallest favour. But if the blessings of the gospel, the greatest as well as the least, are offered to all, notwithstanding their unworthiness; if all are commanded and invited to come and receive them; if the promises are given to all that come; then there can be no presumption in coming.

Away, then, with all such objections and excuses. Resist all such temptations. It is the duty, as well as the happiness, of all to become holy. Therefore, whosoever thou art that readest or hearest this, embrace the opportunity now offered to secure this blessing to thyself. Lay hold on the hope which is now set before thee.— Thou art no intruder. Thy Saviour bids thee come. When he died, he procured holiness and heaven for thee. Yes, for *thee*. When he hung upon the cross, he had his eye fixed upon thee, and he has not lost sight of thee from that time to the present. And now he is saying, "All is thine." If thou excusest thyself, thou wilt grieve him; but if thou approachest his throne boldly, thou will please him, and he will rejoice over thee. Of all the favours he giveth, none are bestowed so cheerfully as holiness. "Therefore ask and receive that your joy may be full." Doest thou say, "But I am too dark, too ignorant, too weak, too full of sin to think of being made holy; surely none ever obtained that blessing, who were so unworthy?" Alas! my brother, how often must thou be told that thou shiftest the ground of thy salvation from *faith* to *works!* If thou art to be sanctified and saved by *works*, then object your unworthiness, till thou art worthy; and then come and demand thy sanctification as thy due. But if thy salvation is the work of God and the gift of his grace, then come as thou art, come with all thy unworthiness, and receive sanctification as a beggar receiveth alms. Thy unworthiness shall give him an opportunity of magnifying his grace, and setting off his mercy to the greatest advantage.

7. Not a few of those who are stirred up to seek full sanctification, are more or less discouraged and hindered by this temptation; that if they obtain the blessing, they shall not be able to keep it. In reply to which it is sufficient to observe, that this would be true if they were required to keep it by their own strength. But this is not the case. They shall be kept "by the power of God through faith unto salvation." And he who is able to sanctify them, is able, also, to preserve them in that state. And he will do it; for "he will not leave them nor forsake them." "I will dwell in them," says he, "and walk in them, and be their God." Our blessed Saviour says, "And my Father will love them, and *we* will come and make our *abode* with them." This is not a transient visit which is here promised, but a settled residence. And no one need to doubt that in whatsoever temple the Triune God dwells, he will keep it in purity and peace.

8. Some are tempted to discouragement from the consideration that they have sought so long and have not obtained. But why should they be discouraged? Has God any where said, that all who seek shall find in the same length of time? Or has he said that all who are to be sanctified, shall obtain that blessing in so many weeks or years? Nay, verily; but it is in this respect as it is in respect of justification, — some seek longer, and some a shorter time, before they obtain. But in neither case does it appear to be appointed that we should seek so many weeks or years before we can come into possession of the object. And did we seek aright, we might as well, for ought [*sic*] that is revealed, obtain in a day as in a year.

The person, therefore, who complains that he has been seeking so long, and has not obtained, would do well to inquire how he has sought; for they who seek aright shall find; but they who do not, shall not "be able to obtain." To assist him in this inquiry, I would ask him *what* he has been seeking? He will doubtless say, "sanctification." But it is possible after all that he is mistaken, that he has been all the while seeking something else under that name. He may have placed sanctification too high, or too low, or he may have placed it in some imaginary or ideal thing; and then it is no wonder that he should not obtain.

If any one would obtain sanctification, he must know that it does not consist in the perfection of knowledge, or in the perfection of our natural powers, in lights or in raptures; but in being delivered from all sinful desires and tempers, and filled with the pure love of God.

If, upon inquiry, he finds that his views of this subject are correct, let him in the next place ask himself whether he has had a conviction of the importance of sanctification, and whether that conviction has produced a firm and steady resolution to go on to perfection? Some people go altogether by impulses and strong impressions upon their minds. Under an exhortation, or in a meeting, you may see them engaged and resolutely set upon taking the kingdom by violence; and the next time you meet with them, they are discouraged, irresolute, and weak as another man. What they gain at one time they lose at another, and thus by going forward and backward, forward and backward, they continue to travel the same ground over and over, and gain no lasting good. If they continue thus to halt in the race, they never will obtain what they seek. To obtain sanctification you must keep your resolution through all trials, inward and outward, and through all that variety of frames and feelings of mind you may have, and persevere against all the temptations of Satan, and the opposition of inbred sin, and even against outward sin if you should at anytime fall into it. If upon examination he finds that this is not the ground on which he has failed, let him inquire again whether he has sought by faith or by works. Some have a zeal for God, but not according to knowledge. "Being ignorant of God's merciful method of sanctifying his people, and going about to establish their own righteousness, as the cause of their sanctification," they have not obtained, and in this way they cannot obtain. They ask God to sanctify them, it is true; but they do not believe he will do it while they are so sinful, and instead of laying hold of the blessing by faith, they are endeavouring to fit themselves to be sanctified.

Once more. Some who believe that sanctification is to be obtained by faith, yet hold that faith in the *Antinomian* or *Solifidian* way, and do not rightly balance faith and works. While some seek by works alone, they seek by faith alone. They ask as though they expected God would infuse sanctification into them, instead of working it in them through their own exertions. It is true, that sanctification is obtained by faith; but then it is a faith which is accompanied by earnest efforts to overcome all sin, and to possess and practice all righteousness. He who would obtain sanctification, must consider what he ought to be, and endeavour after it; and while endeavouring after it with all his might, let him trust wholly in Christ for success. Let him not trust in his own doings, as though they could merit any thing, or render him any more fit or worthy to be sanctified; but let his trust be in the alone merits of Christ. All who fail of complete sanctification, fail on one or another of these grounds: either they seek something else under pretence of seeking sanctification; or they do not seek steadily and perseveringly; or they seek it by works, or by faith without works. And hence they make no advances. They remain in the dark, and are full of perplexities. But let them find out the cause of their ill success, and put it away. When the cause is removed, the effects shall cease.

If, however, their own minds are too much perplexed to discern the cause, let them converse with some judicious friend who can instruct them. Their case is far from being hopeless. The Lord shall appear for them. The "Sun of righteousness shall yet arise upon them, with healing in his wings," and scatter all their darkness and their sin, and fill them with all the fruits of righteousness.

Irregular Exercises in Experience

[The following observations, and directions are chiefly taken from a manuscript Address, by an esteemed brother in the ministry, who was requested to look over my little work before it went to press and who expressed a wish that something of the kind might go into this Manual.]

Inconstancy of mind attends too many Christians. Some, who never had a very satisfactory evidence of their justification, under temptation, become discouraged; and though at times their hope may a little revive, yet in a great degree they remain unsettled in their determinations and faith.

Others who have had the Spirit of adoption, by not walking in Christ as they received him, lose their first love, become involved in darkness, and fear they shall never again enjoy what they have lost. And this fear enervates all their efforts to regain that treasure.

Many did run well for awhile. They obtained many degrees of sanctifying grace— thirsted for full redemption— walked in the light of God's countenance— found delight in self denial and bearing the cross; but, alas! they are hindered; they begin to measure themselves by others, give way to carnal reasoning— listen to the suggestions of Satan, and indulge in reflections like these: "How can I expect the Lord will sanctify my soul, when many, who have had religion longer than I, have not received that blessing? Many preachers say but little about sanctification, and but few profess to enjoy it. Indeed, it appears to be the privilege of but few, and I cannot expect to be one of them. I will do as well as I can, and hope to be sanctified before I die."

There may be others who thought they obtained this state of grace. They felt no sin, and their hearts were filled with love. For some time they could say,

> "Not a cloud doth arise
> To darken my skies,
> Or hide for a moment my Lord from my eyes."

At length some unlooked-for temptation came or some rising of heart they did not expect; when they began to question the reality of the work, and to think they were deceived. The more they pondered upon the subject, the darker they became, till they finally sunk in perplexity and discouragement. Such have sorrow which none knows but he who feels it. If at any time hope a little revives, they are put down by the rush of temptation. It is suggested, "You have done your best, and were deceived. Others have been deceived as well as you. Where are those now who have made this great profession?" &c. These temptations reach to the very centre of the soul. Under them the mind will occasionally make violent efforts, and then relapse into a state of strange indifference. Doubts arise whether they shall ever obtain the forfeited blessing, or if they should, whether they shall be able to hold it.

Murmuring frequently succeeds to fruitless efforts, and such a one is apt to say, "Mine is an uncommon case. I have done all I can, and it avails nothing. It is useless to make any farther effort. It is easy for others to believe, but not for me. I should be willing to do or suffer any thing to obtain the favour of God. But I have no power to do any thing. I make resolutions in sincerity and the fulness of my heart: but I do not keep them."

There is a great deal of unbelief, obstinacy, and accusation, against God, implied, though not intended, in all this. But surely this is not the way to obtain help. These cases, but more especially the last, is strongly marked, and like a complication of bodily diseases, requires strong remedies, and those skillfully applied. The following directions, if properly attended to, will not fail to bring the desired relief.

1. Cease from all murmuring against God as though he required more difficult conditions of thee than of others; and from excusing thyself as though what he required of thee was above thy strength. Hush this clamor in thy soul, that thou mayest hear the voice of God speaking within thee.

2. Hast thou not put thine own "resolutions" and "faithfulness" in the place of faith? Faith may be called the tree, and *faithfulness* the fruit of that tree. How then canst thou expect the fruit without the tree? All resolutions to be more faithful, while faith is wanting, will be ineffectual. *First make the tree good, and the fruit shall be good also.* The heart is a fountain of unclean waters. Faith in Christ has a direct influence upon the fountain to cleanse it. And in vain dost thou attempt to purify the streams while the fountain remains impure. Instead of following that divine influence which would lead you to purify the fountain, thou resolvest to purify the streams, and thus lose thy labour.

Thou must retire within thyself, search thy heart with jealous severity; listen to the voice of God within thee, and cry earnestly to him for light to show thee thy true state, and to direct thee in every step. By this light thou wilt see that thy hasty resolutions to be faithful without faith, grieved his Spirit, by withdrawing thy attention from Christ; and produced no other effect than to quiet the clamours of a guilty conscience for a moment.

Your first care should be to have your backslidings healed and to obtain the evidence of the divine favour, and then in that light go on to perfection.

3. By retiring within, and paying a closer attention to the workings of thy heart, thou mayest be less ready to make fair promises of doing better; And, oppressed with a mass of corruption, thou wilt loathe thyself, and be ready to cry out, "Cleanse thou me from secret faults. Create in me a clean heart, and renew a right spirit within me."

If you follow the order of God, your exercises will become deep and lasting, and for the present they may be painful. Such darkness may be upon your mind, that you may be tempted to doubt whether you ever experienced religion, or ever shall. But while a sense of your depravity, unfaithfulness, and ill desert, is tearing your heart strings asunder, the mercy of God is leading you to the sin-atoning sacrifice.

If you once thought your heart was renewed in love, you may be strongly tempted to think it more difficult for you to regain the blessing, and not so likely to succeed, as though you had never enjoyed it. But this is a mistake. God is as able and willing to restore this blessing, as he is to restore justification to one who has lost it. He does not say, I will justify or sanctify you once and no more; but he has appointed the conditions on which he will both justify and sanctify; and these conditions he will not alter; so that whosoever will, may come and be saved. And remember that sin, when truly repented of, gives you your first title to Christ, and simple faith the second. Come, then, resting on the atonement, throw yourself down at the feet of Christ, and abide in importunate prayer until he comes and rain righteousness upon you.

4. You may possibly say, "My heart does not feel to yield to Christ." But you must consider that he does not require you to walk or to act by feeling, but by faith. Submit your heart to the Saviour on conviction of duty, and obstinately believe, that is, against all temptations and suggestions to the contrary; till all opposition gives way, and your whole soul cries out, "Thy will be done." And *if he tarry, wait for him.* Be not impatient; for he will come in the most suitable time. *Fret not thyself in any wise* because thou canst not see his countenance, hear his voice, taste his love according to thy desire; but continue thy desire and thy expectation unto him as much as possible every moment, till he come and accomplish the good pleasure of his will in thee. Thy circumstances may suggest the meaning, and thy duty, in that command, "Stand still, and see the salvation of the Lord." And so surely as he appeared for the salvation of the Israelites, he will appear for thine.

5. We ought with much simplicity, on proper occasions, to *profess* what God has done for us. But we may be sensible that God wrought a great work in us, without knowing whether it be complete sanctification or not. Yea, one may feel for the present nothing contrary to love, and yet not be completely sanctified. But when he has the full evidence of sanctification, he ought not to speak of it to every one, nor introduce it into common conversation. This would be making too light of it. Besides, many have no eyes to see this doctrine in the gospel, and many Christians are strongly prejudiced against it. To profess sanctification before such would only fill them with rage, and cause them to speak evil of the things they know not. This would be like *casting pearls before swine.*

But when you are with those who would be instructed and edified by it, it will be your duty, in all humility and simplicity, to declare what God has done for you. It then becomes your duty, and you cannot retain the evidence of it if you conceal it.

May the Lord give us all wisdom in all things. May we all watch for the coming of our Lord to sanctify us; and then may we meet in glory and sing together, "Worthy is the Lamb that was slain, and hath washed us in his own blood, to receive honour, and glory, and power, for ever and ever. Amen."

Chapter V.
Evidences and Marks of Christian Perfection

IT IS VERY NECESSARY that the evidence should be added to the work of sanctification, that he who has experienced that work may have the enjoyment of it. Without this, he would be like a person who should have a large estate fall to him; but being ignorant of it, could not have the enjoyment and use of it as though he knew it. The evidence of sanctification may be compared to the key stone which binds and strengthens an arch, or to the last touches of the pencil, which give a polish to the fair picture. We may suppose the work of sanctification, or cleansing from sin, to exist without the evidence, or to be distinct from it; but it would be manifestly unsafe for any one to rest without it.

It is true many have thought they had the evidence of sanctification when they had it not, and have brought dishonour upon the profession of it. This was because they knew not what the evidence is. They judged by false marks. They had received a large measure of love, and were exceedingly joyful; and took these for an evidence of sanctification. Perhaps some, on slighter grounds still, have believed themselves sanctified. — But it is not great love and joy, no, nor the feeling no sin added thereto, that will prove a person thoroughly sanctified; because it is often the case that all these unite in the justified state. Where love and joy are, the motions of sin are, for the time being, suspended, though it remains in the heart.

The evidence of sanctification is twofold, and results, *first*, from the witness of the Spirit of God; and, *secondly*, from the nature of the work.

First. From the witness of the Spirit of God. "We can know that we are sanctified no otherwise than we know we are justified. 'Hereby know we that we are of God,' in either sense, 'by the Spirit he hath given us.' We know it by the 'witness of the Spirit.' As when we were justified, 'the Spirit bore witness with our spirit,' that our sins were forgiven; so when we were sanctified, he bore witness that they were taken away. Indeed the witness of sanctification is not always clear at first, (as neither is that of justification;) neither is it afterwards always the same, but like that of justification, sometimes stronger and sometimes fainter. Yea, and sometimes it is withdrawn. Yet, in general, the latter testimony of the Spirit is both as clear and as steady as that of the former.

"In the hour of temptation Satan clouds the work of God, and injects various doubts and reasonings, especially in those who have either very weak or very strong understandings. At such times there is absolute need of that witness; without which the work of sanctification not only could not be discerned, but could not subsist. Were it not for this, the soul could not then abide in the love of God: much less could it rejoice evermore, and in every thing give thanks. In these circumstances, therefore, a *direct testimony* that we are sanctified, is necessary in the highest degree. And the following Scriptures give reason to expect it: 'We have received not the spirit of the world, but the

Spirit which is of God, that we may know the things that are freely given to us of God,' 1 Cor. ii, 12.

"Now surely sanctification is one of the things which are freely given to us of God. And no possible reason can be assigned why this should be excepted, when the apostle says, 'we receive the Spirit' *for this very end,* 'that we may know the things which are *thus* freely given us.'

"Is not the same thing implied in that well known Scripture, Rom. viii, 16, 'The Spirit itself beareth witness with our spirit, that we are the children of God.' Does he only witness this to those who are children of God in the lowest sense? Nay, but to those also who are such in the highest sense. And does he not witness that they are such in the highest sense? What reason have we to doubt it?

"Consider, likewise, 1 John v, 19, 'We know that we are of God.' *How?* 'By the Spirit he hath given us,' 1 John iii, 24. *Nay,* 'hereby we know that he abideth in us.' And what ground have we, either from Scripture or reason, to exclude the witness any more than the fruit of the Spirit from being here intended? By this then, also, *we know that we are of God,* and *in what sense* we are so. Whether we are babes, young men, or fathers, we know in the same manner.

"Not that I affirm that all young men, or even fathers, have this testimony every moment; there may be intermission of the direct testimony that they are thus born of God. But these intermissions are fewer and shorter as they grow up in Christ. And some have the testimony both of their justification and sanctification, without any intermission at all: which I presume more might have, did they walk as humbly and closely with God as they may."*

Secondly. The evidence of sanctification results from the nature of that state. And here two things may be noticed, the absence of sin, and the fruits of the Spirit.

---

*Wesley's [A] Plain Account [of Christian Perfection].

1. The absence of sin. In the work of sanctification there is such a change wrought in all the affections and tempers of the mind, as effectually to do away every root of bitterness, every evil propensity. Here let the person who would ascertain his true state, take into view the process of the work he has experienced. Has he had a clear discovery of the depravity of his nature? Has he seen and lamented his unlikeness to God, his proneness to wander from God in his thoughts, words, tempers and actions? Has he seen and bewailed the stubbornness of his will, the hardness of his heart, his remaining unbelief, pride, anger, impatience, and a thousand evils of his nature? Has he fled from himself to the Saviour for help? And has he obtained help against all these? Has the Lord Jehovah come to his relief? Are the evils under which he groaned, gone? He says, I feel them not. But are they entirely destroyed, or only suspended? Here let him ask whether a sufficient length of time has elapsed since he felt them, to give them an opportunity to show themselves. In particular, have those occasions and trials occurred which used to excite them? And is there no sense of self will, self applause, anger, impatience, &c, but on the contrary, 2. All the fruits of the Spirit; *love, joy, peace,* always abiding;— *long suffering, patience, resignation;*— *gentleness,* triumphing over all provocation;— *goodness,* mildness, sweetness, tenderness of spirit;— *fidelity,* simplicity, godly sincerity;— *meekness,* calmness, evenness of spirit;— *temperance,* not only in food and drink, but in all things temporal and spiritual? If, I say, there are no motions of sin, but all the fruits of the Spirit continually present in the soul, then there is good reason to believe the work of sanctification is accomplished. But still this cannot be certainly known without the direct witness of the Spirit: that is, it cannot be certainly known that all sin is de-

stroyed, and all the fruits of the Spirit are in the soul. As was observed above, Satan will at times so becloud the work of the Spirit by his temptations, as to create a doubt of the existence of this or that fruit of the Spirit. So, on the other hand, he will sometimes *accuse* the child of God that he has sinned, that he has indulged some sinful desire or propensity: and he cannot always distinguish between temptation and sin, unless he has the direct witness of the Spirit.

"In some cases," says Mr. Wesley, "it is impossible to distinguish without the *direct witness* of the Spirit. But in general, one may distinguish thus:

"One commends me. Here is a temptation to pride; but instantly my soul is humbled before God, and I feel no pride: of which I am as sure as I am that pride is not humility.

"A man strikes me. Here is a temptation to anger. But my heart overflows with love, and I feel no anger at all; of which I am as sure as I am that love and anger are not the same.

"A woman solicits me. Here is a temptation to lust. But in the instant, I shrink back, and feel no desire or lust at all: of which I am perfectly sure.

"Thus it is if I am tempted by a present object; and it is just the same, if, when it is absent, the devil recalls a commendation, an injury, &c, to my mind. In the instant the soul repels the temptation, and remains filled with pure love.

"And the difference is still plainer, when I compare my present state with my past, wherein I felt temptation and corruption too."

But still there will be many cases in which the child of God will not be able to distinguish without the direct witness of the Holy Spirit. And such a case is a painful one. It is painful to lie under an accusation of having offended God, and not know but it is true. And this is not only a case of pain, but of danger. There is danger of his losing his confidence, becoming perplexed, and falling into darkness, if not into despair and open sin.

The witness of the Spirit is, therefore, to be very highly esteemed, and diligently sought after; and knowing that it is the will of God that we should have it, we *may come boldly and ask and receive, that our joy may be full.*

To assist the pious reader in ascertaining his state, I here subjoin an extract from the Rev. Mr. Wesley's sermon on the "Witness of the Spirit," vol. ii, p. 132.

1. "But what is 'the witness of the Spirit?' The original word *marturia*, may be rendered either (as it is in several places,) *the witness*, or less ambiguously, *the testimony*, or *the record:* so it is rendered in our translation, 1 John v, 11, 'This is the record' (the testimony, the sum of what God testifies in all his sacred writings) 'that God hath given to us eternal life, and this life is in his Son.['] The testimony now under consideration, is given by the Spirit of God *to* and *with* our spirit. He is the person testifying. What he testifies to us is, *that we are the children of God.* The immediate result of this testimony is, *the fruit of the Spirit;*" namely, *love, joy, peace, long suffering, gentleness, goodness.* And without these, the testimony itself cannot continue. For it is inevitably destroyed, not only by the commission of any outward sin, or the omission of any known duty, but by giving way to any inward sin: in a word, by whatever grieves the Holy Spirit of God.

2. "I observed many years ago, 'It is hard to find words in the language of men, to explain the deep things of God. Indeed, there are none that will adequately express what the Spirit of God works in his children. But perhaps one might say, (desiring any who are taught of God, to correct, soften or strengthen the expression,) By the *testimony of the Spirit* I mean an inward impression on the

soul, whereby the Spirit of God immediately and directly witnesses to my spirit that I am a *child of God*, that *Jesus Christ hath loved me, and given himself for me*. That all my sins are blotted out, and I, even I, am reconciled to God,' or cleansed from all sin, and fully renewed in the image of God.

3. "After twenty years farther consideration, I see no cause to retract any part of this. Neither do I conceive how any of these expressions may be altered, so as to make them more intelligible. I can only add, that if any of the children of God will point out any other expressions, which are more clear, or more agreeable to the word of God, I will readily lay these aside.

4. "Mean time let it be observed, I do not mean hereby, that the Spirit of God testifies this by any outward voice: no, nor always by an inward voice, although he may do this sometimes. Neither do I suppose that he always applies to the heart, (though he often may,) one or more texts of Scripture. But he so works upon the soul by his immediate influence, and by a strong, though inexplicable, operation, that the stormy wind and troubled waves subside, and there is a sweet calm: the heart resting, as in the arms of Jesus, and the sinner being clearly satisfied that God is reconciled, that all his iniquities are forgiven," and that he is cleansed from all sin.

5. "Now, what is the matter of dispute concerning this? Not, whether there be a witness or testimony of the spirit? Nor, whether the Spirit does testify with our spirit, that we are the children of God? None can deny this without flatly contradicting the Scriptures, and charging a lie upon the God of truth. Therefore, that there is a testimony of the Spirit, is acknowledged by all parties.

6. "Neither is it questioned, whether there is an indirect *witness* or testimony, that we are the children of God. This is nearly, if not exactly, the same with *the testimony of a good conscience towards God;* and is the result of reason and reflection, on what we feel in our own souls. Strictly speaking it is a conclusion drawn partly from the word of God, and partly from our own experience. The word of God says, every one who has the fruit of the Spirit is a child of God. Experience, or inward consciousness, tells me, that I have the fruit of the Spirit. And hence I rationally conclude, therefore I am a child of God. This is likewise allowed on all hands, and so is no matter of controversy.

7. "Nor do we assert that there can be any real testimony of the Spirit, without the fruits. We assert, on the contrary, that the fruit of the Spirit immediately springs from this testimony: not always, indeed, in the same degree, even when the testimony is first given. And much less afterwards; neither joy, nor peace, are always at one stay. No, nor love; as neither is the testimony itself always equally strong and clear.

8. "That *the testimony of the Spirit of God* must, in the very nature of things, *be antecedent to the testimony of our own spirit* may appear from this single consideration: we must be holy in heart and life, before we can be conscious that we are so. But we must love God before we can be holy at all: this being the root of all holiness. Now we cannot love God, till we know he loves us; *we love him because he first loved us.* And we cannot know his love to us, till his Spirit witnesses it to our spirit. Till then we cannot believe it. We cannot say, *the life which I now live, I live by faith in the Son of God, who loved me, and gave himself for me.* —

> 'Then, only then, we feel
> Our interest in his blood,
> And cry with joy unspeakable,
> Thou art my Lord, my God.'

"Since, then, the testimony of his Spirit must precede the love of God and all holiness, of consequence it must precede our consciousness thereof.

9. "And here properly comes in to confirm this Scriptural doctrine, the experience of the children of God; the experience, not of two or three, not of a few, but of a great multitude which no man can number. It has been confirmed, both in this and in all ages, by a *cloud* of living and dying *witnesses*. It is confirmed by *your* experience and *mine*. The Spirit itself bore witness to my spirit, that I was a child of God, gave me an evidence hereof, and I immediately cried, *Abba, Father!* And this I did (and so did you) before I reflected on, or was conscious of, any fruit of the Spirit. It was from this testimony received, that love, joy, peace, and the whole fruit of the Spirit flowed. First, I heard,
> 'Thy sins are forgiven! accepted thou art!
> I listen'd and heaven sprung up in my heart.'"

The above was written more especially in reference to justification; but it is equally true with respect to sanctification, that the "witness," or testimony, of the Spirit is an inward impression on the soul, whereby he immediately and directly witnesses to my spirit, that I am sanctified, cleansed from all sin, and wholly set apart for God. There is in sanctification, as well as in justification, the twofold witness, that of the Spirit of God, and that of our own spirit. The latter is "nearly, if not exactly, the same with the testimony of a good conscience towards God: and is the result of reason or reflection on what we feel in our own souls. Strictly speaking, it is a conclusion drawn partly from the word of God, and partly from our own experience. The word of God says, every one who has the perfect fruit of the Spirit, is a sanctified child of God. Experience, or inward consciousness, tells me, that I have this fruit of the Spirit. And hence I rationally conclude, therefore I am a sanctified child of God."

But the witness of the Spirit of God must go before the witness or testimony of our own spirit, as may be made to appear, thus: "We must be perfectly holy in heart and life, before we can be conscious that we are so. But in order to be perfectly holy, we must love God with all our heart. Now we cannot love God with all the heart, till we know that he hath loved us, and cleansed us from all our sins. And we cannot know that he has loved us, and cleansed us from all sin, till his Spirit witnesses it to our spirit. Till then we cannot believe it.

> Then, only then, we feel
> Perfection in his blood,
> And cry with joy unspeakable,
> ["]Thou art my *all*, my *God.*"

Chapter VI.
Advice to Those Who Profess Christian Perfection[72]

1. "WATCH AND PRAY CONTINUALLY against pride. If God has cast it out, see that it enter no more: It is full as dangerous as desire; and you may slide back into it unawares: especially if you think there is no danger of it. 'Nay, but I ascribe all I have to God.' So you may, and be proud nevertheless. For it is pride, not only to ascribe any thing we have to ourselves, but to think we have what we really have not. You ascribe all the knowledge you have to God; and in this respect you are humble. But if you think you have more than you really have: or if you think you are so taught of God, as no longer to need man's teaching, pride lieth at the door.

"Do not, therefore, say to any who would advise or reprove you, 'you are blind: you cannot teach *me*.' Do not say, 'this is your *wisdom*, your *carnal reason*,' but calmly weigh the thing before God.

---

72. This entire chapter is taken from Wesley's *A Plain Account of Christian Perfection*.

"Always remember, much grace does not imply much light. These do not always go together. As there may be much light where there is little love, so there may be much love where there is little light. The heart has more heat than the eye; yet it cannot see. And God has wisely tempered the members of the body together, that none may say to another, 'I have no need of thee.'

"To imagine none can teach you, but those who are themselves saved from sin, is a very great and dangerous mistake. Give not place to it for a moment. It will lead you into a thousand mistakes, and that irrecoverably. *Obey and regard them who are over you in the Lord;* and do not think you know better than they. Know their place, and *your own:* always remembering, much love does not imply much light.

"The not observing this has led some into many mistakes, and into the appearance, at least, of pride. Oh! beware of the appearance and of the thing. Let there *be in you that* lowly *mind which was in Jesus Christ.* And *be ye* likewise *clothed with humility.* Let it not only fill but cover you all over. Let modesty and self diffidence appear in all your words and actions. Let all you speak and do, show that you are little, and base, and mean, and vile, in your own eyes.

"As one instance of this, be always ready to own any fault you have done. If you have at any time thought, spoke, or acted wrong, be not backward to acknowledge it. Never dream that this will hurt the cause of God; no, it will farther it. Be, therefore, open and frank when you are taxed with any thing: do not seek either to evade or disguise it. But let it appear just as it is, and you will thereby not hinder, but adorn the gospel.

2. "Beware of that daughter of pride, *enthusiasm!* keep at the utmost distance from it: give no place to a heated imagination. Do not hastily ascribe things to God. Do

not easily suppose dreams, voices, impressions, visions, or revelations, to be from God. They may be from him; they may be from nature: they may be from the devil. Therefore *believe not every spirit, but try the spirits whether they be from God.* Try all things by the written word, and let all bow down before it. You are in danger of enthusiasm every hour, if you depart ever so little from Scripture, yea, from the plain, literal meaning of any text, taken in connection with the context. And so you are, if you despise or lightly esteem reason, knowledge, or human learning: every one of which is an excellent gift of God, and may serve the noblest purposes.

"I advise you never to use the words, *wisdom, reason,* or *knowledge,* by way of reproach. On the contrary, pray that you yourself may abound in them more and more. If you mean *worldly* wisdom, *useless* knowledge, *false* reasoning, say so; and throw away the chaff, but not the wheat.

"One general inlet to enthusiasm is, expecting the end without the means; the expecting knowledge, for instance, without searching the Scriptures, and consulting the children of God: the expecting spiritual strength, without constant prayer and steady watchfulness: the expecting any blessing without hearing the word of God at every opportunity.

"Some have been ignorant of this device of Satan. They have left off searching the Scriptures. They said, 'God writes all the Scriptures on my heart; therefore I have no need to read them.'* Others thought they had not so much need of hearing, and so grew slack in attending preaching. Oh! take warning, you who are concerned herein. You have listened to the voice of a stranger. Fly back to Christ, and keep in the good old way, which was *once delivered to the saints.*

"The very desire of *growing in grace* may sometimes

---

*I have not known any of those who have experienced sanctification among us of late who have done thus. But, because there is danger, beware!

be an inlet of enthusiasm. As it constantly leads us to seek *new grace*, it may lead us, unawares, to seek something else new, besides *new degrees* of love to God and man. So it has led some to fancy they had received gifts of a *new kind* after a new heart, as, 1, The loving God with all the mind; 2, with all the soul; 3, with all the strength; 4, oneness with God; 5, oneness with Christ; 6, having their lives hid with Christ in God; 7, the being dead with Christ; 8, risen with him; 9, the sitting with him in heavenly places; 10, the being taken up into his throne; 11, the being in the New Jerusalem; 12, the seeing the tabernacle of God come down among men; 13, the being dead to all works; 14, the not being liable to death, pain, grief, or temptation; 15, the being in the different states of Christ successively, as his infancy, manhood, sufferings, exaltation, &c.

"One ground of many of these mistakes is, the taking every fresh, strong application of any of these Scriptures to the heart, to be a gift of a new kind: not knowing that several of these Scriptures are not fulfilled yet; that most of the others were fulfilled when we were justified; the rest the moment we are sanctified. It remains only to experience them in higher degrees: this is all we have to expect.

"Another ground of these and a thousand mistakes is, the not considering deeply, that love is the highest gift of God, humble, gentle, patient love: that all visions, revelations, manifestations whatever, are little things compared to love; and that all the gifts above mentioned are the same with, or infinitely inferior to it.

"It were well you should be thoroughly sensible of this: the heaven of heavens is love. There is nothing higher in religion: there is, in effect, nothing else: if you look for any thing but *more love*, you are looking wide of the mark, you are getting out of the royal way. And when you are asking others, have you received this or that blessing? if you mean any thing but *more love*, you are wrong: you are leading them out of the way, and putting them upon a false scent. Settle it then in your heart, that from the moment God has saved you from your sins, you are to aim at nothing more, but more of that love described in the thirteenth of the first epistle to the Corinthians. You can go no higher than, this till you are carried into Abraham's bosom.

"I say again, beware of *enthusiasm*. Such as the imagining you have the gift of prophesying, or of discerning spirits, which I do not believe one of you has; no, nor ever had yet. Beware of judging people to be either right or wrong, by your own feelings. This is no scriptural way of judging. Oh keep close to the law, and to the testimony.

3. "Beware of *Antinomianism*, the 'making void the law,' or any part of it, 'through faith.' Enthusiasm naturally leads to this; indeed they scarce can be separated. This may steal upon you in a thousand forms, so that you cannot be too watchful against it. Take heed of every thing, whether in principle or practice, which has any tendency thereto. Even that great truth, that 'Christ is the end of the law,' may betray us into it, if we do not consider that he has adopted every point of the moral law, and grafted it into the law of love. Beware of thinking, 'because I am filled with love, I need not have so much holiness: because I pray always, therefore I need no set time for private prayer: because I watch always, therefore I need no particular self examination.' Let us 'magnify the law,' the whole written word, 'and make it honourable.' Let this be our voice, 'I prize thy commandments above gold or precious stones. Oh what love have I unto thy law. All the day long is my study in it.' Beware of *Antinomian books*. They contain many excellent things; and this makes them the more dangerous. Oh be warned

in time! do not play with fire; do not put your hand on the hole of a cockatrice den! I entreat you, beware of *bigotry*. Let not your love or beneficence be confined to Methodists only; much less to that very small part of them, who seem to be renewed in love: or to those who believe yours and their report. Oh make this not your *Shibboleth!* Beware of *stillness:* ceasing in a wrong sense from your own works. To mention one instance out of many:— 'You have received,' says one, 'a great blessing: but you began to talk of it, and to do this and that: so you lost it. You should have been still.'

"Beware of *self indulgence:* yea, and making a virtue of it, laughing at *self denial* and taking up the cross daily, at fasting or abstinence. Beware of *censoriousness*, thinking or calling them that any wise oppose you, whether in judgment or practice, blind, dead, fallen, or 'enemies to the work.' Once more, beware of *Solifidianism;* crying nothing but 'believe, believe:' and condemning those as ignorant or legal, who speak in a more spiritual way. At certain seasons, indeed, it may be right to treat of nothing but repentance, or merely of faith, or altogether of holiness: but in general our call is, to declare the whole counsel of God, and to prophesy according to the analogy of faith. The written word treats of the whole, and every particular branch of righteousness, descending to its minutest branches, as, to be sober, courteous, diligent, patient, to honour all men. So likewise the Holy Spirit works the same in our hearts, not merely creating desires after holiness in general, but strongly inclining us to every particular grace, and leading us to every individual part of 'whatsoever is lovely.' And this with the greatest propriety; for as by 'works faith is made perfect,' so the completing or destroying the work of faith, and enjoying the favour, or suffering the displeasure of God, greatly depends on every single act of obedience or disobedience.

4. "Beware of *sins of omission:* lose no opportunity of doing good in any kind. Be zealous of good works. Willingly omit no work, either of piety or mercy. Do all the good you possibly can to the bodies and souls of men; particularly 'thou shalt in anywise reprove thy neighbour, and not suffer sin upon him.' Be *active.* Give no place to indolence or sloth: give no occasion to say, 'ye are idle, ye are idle.' Many will say so still; but let your whole behavior refute the slander. Be always employed; lose no shred of time; gather up the fragments, that none be lost; and whatsoever thy hand findeth to do, do it with thy might. Be *slow* to *speak,* and wary in speaking. 'In a multitude of words there wanteth not sin.' Do not talk much, neither long at a time. Few can converse profitably above an hour. Keep at the utmost distance from pious chit-chat, from religious gossiping.

5. "Beware of *desiring* anything but God, now you desire nothing else. Every other desire is driven out; see that none enter again. 'Keep thyself pure, let your eye' remain 'single, and your whole body shall be full of light. Admit no desire of pleasing food, or any other pleasure of sense; no desire of pleasing the eye or the imagination, by any thing grand, or new, or beautiful; no desire of money, of praise, or esteem, of happiness in *any creature.* You *may* bring these desires back, but you need not, you need feel them no more. Oh 'stand fast in the liberty wherewith Christ hath made you free.' Be patterns to all of denying yourselves, and taking up your cross daily. Let them see that you make no account of any pleasure which does not bring you nearer to God; nor regard any pain which does; that you simply aim at pleasing him, whether by doing or suffering; that the constant language of your heart with regard to pleasure or pain, honour or dishonour, riches or poverty, is

'All's alike to me, so I
In my Lord may live and die.'

6. "Beware of *schism*, of making a rent in the church of Christ. That inward disunion, the members ceasing to have reciprocal love one for another, 1 Cor. xii, 25, is the very root of all contention, and every outward separation. Beware of every thing tending thereto. Beware of a dividing spirit; shun whatever has the least aspect that way. Therefore say not, 'I am of Paul, or of Apollos;'— the very thing that occasioned the schism at Corinth. Say not, 'this is my preacher— the best preacher in England; give me him, and take all the rest.' All this tends to breed or foment division, to disunite those whom God hath joined. Do not run down any preacher. Do not exalt one above the rest, lest you hurt both him and the cause of God. On the other hand, do not bear hard upon any by reason of some incoherency, or inaccuracy of expression; no, nor for some mistakes, were they really such.

"Likewise if you would avoid schism, observe every *rule* of the *society*, and of the *bands* for conscience' sake. Never omit meeting your class or band; never absent yourself from any public meeting: these are the very sinews of our society, whatever tends to weaken our regard for these, or our exactness in attending them, strikes at the very root of our community. As one saith, 'That part of our economy, the private weekly meetings for prayer, examination, and particular exhortation, has been the greatest means of deepening and continuing every blessing that was received by the word preached, and of diffusing it to others who could not attend the public ministry— whereas, without this religious conversation and intercourse, the most ardent attempts by mere preaching, have proved of little lasting use.'

"Suffer not one thought of separating from your brethren, whether their opinions agree with yours or not. Do not dream that any man sins in not believing *you*, in not taking *your word;* or that this or that opinion is essential to the work, and both must stand or fall together. Beware of *impatience of contradiction.* Do not condemn or think hardly of those who cannot see just as you see, or who judge it their duty to contradict you, whether in a great thing or a small. I fear some of us have thought hardly of others, merely because they contradicted what we affirmed. All this tends to division; and by every thing of this kind, we are teaching them an easy lesson against ourselves. 'Oh beware of touchiness, of testiness, not bearing to be spoken to, starting at the least word, and flying from those who do not implicitly receive mine or another's sayings!'

"Expect contradiction and opposition, together with crosses of various kinds. Consider the words of St. Paul, 'To you it is given in the behalf of Christ,' for his sake, as a fruit of his death and intercession for you, 'not only to believe, but also to suffer for his sake,' Phil. i, 29. *It is given!* God *gives* you this opposition or reproach; it is a fresh token of his love. And will you disown the giver? or spurn his gift, and count it a misfortune? Will you not rather say, 'Father, the hour is come that thou shouldest be glorified. Now thou givest thy child to suffer something for thee. Do with me according to thy will.[']

"Know that these things, far from being hinderances to the work of God, or to your soul, unless by your own fault, are not only unavoidable in the course of Providence, but profitable, yea, necessary for you. Therefore receive them from God, (not from chance) with willingness and thankfulness. Receive them from men with humility, meekness, yieldingness, gentleness, sweetness. Why should not even your outward *appearance* and *manner,* be soft? Remember the character of lady Cutts: 'It was said of the Roman emperor, Titus, never any one came displeased *from him*; but it might be said of her, never anyone went displeased to her. So secure were all, of the kind and favourable reception which they should meet with from her.'

"Beware of tempting others to separate from *you*. Give no offense which can possibly be avoided: see that your practice be in all things suitable to your profession, adorning the gospel of God our Saviour. Be particularly careful in speaking of yourself; you may not indeed deny the work of God: but speak of it, when you are called thereto, in the most inoffensive manner possible. Avoid all magnificent, pompous words. Indeed you need give it no *general* name: neither 'perfection, sanctification, the second blessing, nor the having attained.' Rather speak of the particulars which God has wrought for you. You may say, "at such a time I felt a change which I am not able to express. And since that time I have not felt pride, or self will, or wrath, or unbelief: nor any thing but a fulness of love to God and to all mankind.' And answer any other plain question that is asked, with modesty and simplicity.

"And if any of you should at any time fall from what you now are: if you should again feel pride or unbelief, or any temper from which you are now delivered; do not deny, do not hide, do not disguise, it at all, at the peril of your soul. At all events go to one in whom you can confide, and speak just what you feel. God will enable him to speak a word in season, which shall be health to your soul. And surely the Lord will again lift up your head, and cause the bones which have been broken to rejoice.

7. "Be *exemplary* in all things: particularly in outward things, as in dress; in little things, as the laying out of your money, avoiding every needless expense; in deep, steady seriousness, and in the solidity and usefulness of all your conversation. So shall you be 'lights shining in a

dark place:' so shall you daily grow in grace, till 'an entrance be ministered unto you abundantly, into the everlasting kingdom of our Lord Jesus Christ.'" —*Plain Acc. of Christ. Perfection.*

Chapter VII.
Reflections Chiefly Designed for the Use of Those Who Profess Christian Perfection

Most of the following advices are strongly enforced in the "following reflections, which I recommend," says Mr. Wesley, "to your deep and frequent consideration, next to the Holy Scriptures." —*Plain Account of Christian Perfection.*

1. THE SEA IS AN excellent figure of the fulness of God and that of the blessed Spirit. For as the rivers all run into the sea, so the bodies, the souls, and the good works of the righteous, return unto God, to live there in eternal repose.

Although all the graces of God depend on his mere bounty, yet is he pleased generally to attach them to the prayers, the instructions, and the holiness of those with whom we are. By strong, though invisible attractions, he draws some souls by their intercourse with others.

The sympathies formed by grace far surpass those formed by nature.

The truly devout, show that passions as naturally flow

from true as from false love, so deeply sensible are they of the goods and evils of those whom they love for God's sake. But this can only be comprehended by those who understand the language of love.

The bottom of the soul may be in repose even while we are in many outward troubles; just as the bottom of the sea is calm while the surface is strongly agitated? [*sic*]

2. The *best helps to growth in grace,* are the ill usage, the affronts, and the losses which befall us. We should receive them with all thankfulness, as preferable to all others, were it only on this account, that our will has no part therein.

The readiest way to escape from our sufferings, is to be willing they should endure as long as God pleases.

If we suffer persecution and affliction in a right manner, we attain a larger measure of conformity to Christ by a due improvement of one of the occasions, than we could have done merely by imitating his mercy in abundance of good works.

One of the greatest evidences of God's love to those that love him, is to send the afflictions with grace to bear them.

Even in great afflictions, we ought to testify to God, that in receiving them from his hand, we feel pleasure in the midst of the pain, from being afflicted by him who loves us, and whom we love.

The readiest way which God takes to draw a man to himself, is to afflict him in that he loves most, and with good reason; and to cause this affliction to arise from some good action done with a single eye: because nothing can more clearly show him the emptiness of what is most lovely and desirable in the world.

3. True *resignation* consists in a thorough conformity to the whole will of God; who wills and does all (sin excepted) which comes to pass in the world. In order

to this, we have only to embrace all events, good and bad, as his will.

In the greatest afflictions which can befall the just, either from heaven or earth, they remain immovable in peace, and perfectly submissive to God, by an inward, loving regard to him, uniting in one all the powers of their souls.

We ought quietly to suffer whatever befalls us, to bear the defects of others and our own, to confess them to God in secret prayer or with groans which cannot be uttered; but never to speak a sharp or peevish word, nor to murmur or repine.

Be thoroughly willing that God should treat you in the manner that pleases him. We are his lambs, and therefore ought to be ready to suffer, even to death, without complaining.

We are to bear with those we cannot amend, and to be content with offering them to God. This is true resignation. And since he has borne our infirmities, we may well bear those of each other for his sake.

To abandon all, to strip one's self of all in order to seek and to follow Jesus Christ, naked to Bethlehem, where he was born; naked to the hall where he was scourged; and naked to Calvary, where he died on the cross, is so great a mercy, that neither the thing, nor the knowledge of it is given to any, but through faith in the Son of God.

4. There is no love of God without patience, and no patience, without *lowliness* and sweetness of spirit.

Humility and patience are the surest proofs of the increase of love.

Humility alone unites patience with love, without which it is impossible to draw profit from suffering; or indeed to avoid complaint, especially when we think we have given no occasion for what men make us suffer.

True humility is a kind of self annihilation; and this is the centre of all virtues.

A soul returned to God ought to be attentive to every thing which is said to him, on the head of salvation, with a desire to profit thereby.

5. The bearing with men, and suffering evils in meekness and silence, is a grand part of the Christian life.

God is the first object of our love: its next office is, to bear the defects of others. And we should begin the practice of this amidst our own household.

We should particularly exercise our love towards them who most shock either our way of thinking, or our temper, or our knowledge, or the desire we have that others should be as virtuous as we wish to be ourselves.

6. On every occasion of uneasiness, we should retire to prayer, that we may give place to the grace and light of God: and then form our resolutions, without being in any pain about what success they may have.

God's command to "pray without ceasing," is founded on the necessity we have of his grace to preserve the life of God in the soul, which can no more subsist one moment without it than the body can without air.

Prayer continues in the desire of the heart, though the understanding be employed on outward things.

In souls filled with love, the desire to please God is a continual prayer.

As the furious hate which the devil bears us, is termed the roaring of the lion, so our vehement love may be termed, crying after God.

7. It is scarce conceivable how "straight the way" is, wherein God leads them that follow him; and how dependant [sic] on him we must be, unless we are wanting in our faithfulness to him.

It is hardly credible of how great consequence before God, are the smallest things: and what great inconveniences sometimes follow those which appear to be light faults.

As a very little dust will disorder a clock, and the least sand will obscure our sight, so the least grain of sin which is upon the heart, will hinder its right motion towards God.

We should be in the church as the saints are in heaven, and in the house as the holiest men are in the church: doing our work in the house as we pray in the church, worshipping God from the ground of the heart.

We should be continually labouring to cut off all the useless things that surround us. And God usually retrenches the superfluities of our souls, in the same proportion as we do those of our bodies.

The best means of resisting evil, is to destroy whatever of the world remains in us; in order to raise for God, upon its ruins, a building all of love. Then shall we begin in this fleeting life, to love God as we shall love him in eternity.

We scarce conceive how easy it is to rob God of his due, in our friendship with the most virtuous persons, until they are torn from us by death. But if this loss produces lasting sorrow, that is a clear proof that we had before two treasures, between which we divided our hearts.

8. If after having renounced all, we do not watch earnestly, and beseech God to accompany our vigilance with his, we shall be again entangled and overcome.

As the most dangerous winds may enter at little openings, so the devil never enters more dangerously than by little, unobserved incidents, which seem to be nothing, yet insensibly open the heart to great temptations.

It is good to *examine closely* the state of our souls, as if we had never done it before. For nothing tends more to the full assurance of faith, than to keep ourselves by this means in humility, and the exercise of all good works.

To continual watchfulness and prayer, ought to be added continual employment. For grace flies a vacuum as well as nature, and the devil fills whatever God does not fill.

There is no faithfulness like that which ought to be between a guide of souls, and the person directed by him. They ought continually to regard each other in God, and closely to examine themselves, whether all their thoughts are pure, and all their works directed with Christian discretion. Other affairs are only the things of men, but these are peculiarly the things of God.

9. The words of St. Paul, "No man can call Jesus Lord, but by the Holy Ghost," show us the necessity of eyeing God in our *good works,* and even in our minutest thoughts, knowing that none are pleasing to him but those which he forms in us and with us. From hence we learn that we cannot serve him, unless we use our tongue, hands, and heart, to do by his Spirit whatever he would have us do.

If we were not utterly impotent, our good works would be our own property: whereas now they belong wholly to God, because they proceed from him and his grace; while raising our works, and making them all divine, he honours himself in us through them.

One of the principal rules of religion is to lose no occasion of serving God. And since he is invisible to our eyes, we are to serve him in our neighbour; which he receives as if done to himself in person standing visible before us.

God does not love inconstancy in men. Nothing is pleasing to him but what has a resemblance of his own immutability.

A constant attention to the work which God entrusts us with, is a mark of solid piety.

Love fasts when it can, and as much as it can, consistently with health. It leads to all the ordinances of God, and employs itself in all the outward marks whereof it is capable. It flies, as it were like Elijah, over the plain, to find God upon his holy mountain.

God is so great, that he communicates greatness to the least thing that is done for his service.

Happy are they who are sick; yea, or lose their life for having done a good work.

God frequently conceals the part which his children have in the conversion of other souls. Yet one may boldly say, that person who long groans before him for the conversion of another, whenever that soul is converted to God, is one of the chief causes of it.

Charity cannot be practiced right, unless, first, we exercise it the moment God gives the occasion; and then offer it to God by humble thanksgiving. And this for three reasons: 1st. To render to him what we have received from him; 2dly. To avoid the dangerous temptation which springs from the very goodness of these works; and 3rdly. To unite ourselves to God, in whom the soul expands itself in prayer, with all the graces we have received, and the good works we have done, to draw from him new strength against the bad effects which these very works may produce in us, if we do not make use of the antidotes which God has ordained against them. The true means to be filled anew with the riches of grace, is thus to strip ourselves of it: and without this, it is extremely difficult not to grow faint in the practice of good works.

Good works do not receive their last perfection till they, as it were, lose themselves in God. This is a kind of death to them, resembling that of our bodies, which will not gain their highest life, their immortality, till they lose themselves in the glory of our souls, or rather in God, wherewith they shall be filled. And it is only what they had of earthly and mortal, which good works lose by this spiritual death.

Fire is the symbol of love, and the love of God is the principal, and the end of all our good works: but as truth surpasses figure, the fire of divine love has this advantage over material fire, that it can reascend to its source, and raise thither with it all the good works which it produces; and by this means it prevents their being corrupted by pride, vanity, or any evil mixture. But this cannot be done otherwise than by making these good works in a spiritual manner die in God, by a deep gratitude, which plunges the soul in him as in an abyss, with all that it is, and all the grace and good works for which it is indebted to him: a gratitude whereby the soul seems to empty itself of them, that they may return to their source, as rivers seem willing to empty themselves, when they pour themselves with all their waters into the sea.

When we have received any favour from God, we ought to retire, if not into our closets, into our hearts, and say, "I come, Lord, to restore to thee what thou hast given, and I freely relinquish it, to enter again into my own nothingness. For what is the most perfect creature in heaven or in earth in thy presence, but a void capable of being filled with thee and by thee, as the air which is void and dark, is capable of being filled with the light of the sun? Grant, therefore, oh Lord, that I may never appropriate thy grace to myself, any more than the air appropriates to itself the light of the sun, which withdraws it every day to restore it the next, there being nothing in the air that either appropriates its light or resists it. Oh give me the same facility of receiving and restoring thy grace and good works! I say thine: for I acknowledge the root from which they spring is in thee, and not in me."

VII. REFLECTIONS CHIEFLY DESIGNED FOR THOSE WHO PROFESS CHRISTIAN PERFECTION

The following reflections, designed as "Helps to a Growth in Grace," are from a correspondent of the author's, and are worthy the attention of all who are aiming at Christian perfection.

1. To be deeply sensible that we deserve no blessing from the hand of God, and that all we enjoy is the fruit of his mere love and mercy.

Self love inclines us to complain if we are not comfortable and happy; this disposition prevents our enjoying what we really possess, and which, by a right use, would be a means of encouragement.

2. To know that whatever others are, or are not, whatever they do, or do not, *our* duty is to serve God to the extent of the faculties he has given us.

Many hinder the progress of the work in their own souls by reflecting on others as the cause of their unhappiness, and by thinking their outward circumstances must be changed before they can grow in grace.

3. To love without partiality all the children of God as members of the body of Christ, though they be poor, or have a more obscure or humble office to perform, or do not jointly agree with us in sentiment or practice, is also an imperious duty.

A partiality for some particular person or persons, because we find in them a similarity of sentiment which strengthens our own views and choice, and an aversion to others who do not thus coincide with us, has often grieved the Holy Spirit, and hindered his work in the soul.

4. The first step to an increase of knowledge is to be sensible that we are ignorant. To think we already, know fixes an impassable barrier to advancement.

To think we have attained a higher state of grace than

is really the case, is to lower our aims, and prevent ourselves from aspiring to that excellence which we should by raising the standard higher.

5. When peculiarly favoured with divine manifestations, consider them not as the *chief good*; but as a ray only of that refulgence which proceeds from the Fountain of light, and which is given as a conductor to the Fountain itself.

Thinking too much of the great blessings we have received may darken the mind; enraptured with the gift we undervalue the Giver, till he withdraws himself for a season, to show us that without Him we are nothing.

6. We should speak with caution of our experience, both as to time and manner, keeping Christ continually in view: which we cannot do without a forgetfulness of ourselves.

Speaking frequently and indiscriminately of our attainments, though apparently designed to do good, has often some view of self connected with it, by which we would appear wonderful proficients in religion, as being so remarkably distinguished in our experience.

7. If we would follow Christ *fully*, we must be willing to be thought *fools* for his sake; not only by gainsayers, but by such as have honoured our former testimony and conduct with their belief and approbation.

It is a hinderance to the work in us, if we are unwilling that our faith, design, or practice, should be judged erroneous, and have a strong desire that others should see in our light, and acquiesce in our views. We should consider that God deals differently with different persons, and differently with the same person at different times, as their different states require.

8. We should consider that, notwithstanding we have grace, we may have much ignorance. To pretend to know the designs of God respecting ourselves or others, savours strongly of presumption. With him the wisdom of men is foolishness, and their strength weakness. When we lose all desire to be *something ourselves* in religion, we shall be in a situation to glorify God the most perfectly in any way.

People often err by thinking that extraordinary grace conferred on themselves or others, qualifies for extraordinary usefulness in their own prescribed way: not considering that God may be glorified in ways which our conceptions do not reach, and in ways which to us appear unlikely.

9. "To do good, and to communicate, forget not:" but never let the imagination run upon doing what is out of your power to do: for in this way we waste a talent of time which should *now* be employed for God, and the grace which was designed for our own improvement, is bestowed to no purpose.

10. We should think less of what we are in the view of others, than of what we are in our own or in the view of God. If any commend us, let their ignorance of our imperfections excite our pity rather than our vanity. Spiritual vanity is of all the most abhorred in the eyes of judicious persons, as well as in the eyes of perfect purity. If we have grace, it will appear best without our taking pains to have it known.

There is danger in being thought deeply pious. While the mind is taken up with the supposed opinion of others, it wishes to confirm that opinion, to which end it often takes steps out of the right order of things, and becomes more obscure when it would fain give more light.

11. We must "pray with all manner of prayer and supplication in the Spirit," considering the Lord always present. And we can pray, though in company or business which we could not well dispense with for retirement. It is the want of this spirit which makes us groan for relief from care and company. We can be as much with God in one place as in another. Many go to their prayers, with such a load as takes them nearly all the length of their devotions to lay off, and if they get rid of it, think they do well. But this does not carry them forward; it only brings up old arrearages. But constant prayer keeps the mind even; and stated opportunities then will be real furtherances.

But some Christians restrict too much their ideas of prayer to *time, form,* and *attitude;* by a strict attention to which, the intervals are often considered as relaxations from the *spirit* of *devotion,* and are spent carelessly if no worse.

12. We should consider trials and temptations profitable by exercising grace, or showing us the want of it. The only way of rectifying mistakes, is humbly to submit to the pain they give us, and give them up to the Lord. To be pardoned and freed from them, rest solely on the merits of Christ and the aid of the Holy Spirit; and not on any skill derived from past experience.

When trials and temptations come, to seek relief in any way other than resignation; or when overcome with real faults, to set about a rectification of them ourselves, without feeling suitably our dependance on divine mercy, is only to make a bad matter worse.

13. We should follow no custom, and continue no practice, because we have done it, or people expect it of us; unless it be productive of present good to ourselves or others, or is likely so to be.

14. Let the mind run upon no object or fancied circumstances, which even religion might tolerate. Be satisfied to know that the things which are best for us shall be given us: and that we have nothing to do with any other.

To associate in our ideas, circumstances which we could wish to take place, if they would not violate the rules of religion; or to contemplate a subject with which we are not connected, though in itself proper, is to dissipate the mind, and throw away the time which is thus spent.

15. Resolve that none of our happiness shall consist in eating and drinking, or in any of the pleasures of sense. Use nothing of those but that they may fit us for the better service of God; and by examining whether they do, we shall be able to judge how far they are lawful.

An unlawful indulgence to any of the senses, invariably weakens or blunts the spiritual appetite. Some, after keeping themselves under for a while, loose the reigns [sic], and grant liberty equal to a compromise, for their temporary privation; and their last state becomes worse than the first.

16. In whatever state we are, if we would advance, we must *now* direct the first step for that purpose. We may for ever complain of trials if we do not follow the dictates of grace and reason.

To design an improvement in heart or life, without making the present time conducive to it, is to see our faults and yet persist in them. Delaying the work is a sure way of its never being accomplished.

17. Let no reflections on the past good or ill of life, prevent giving the present moment to Christ.

Not giving up entirely all our former experiences, whether good or bad, and limiting all reflections upon our own or others' conduct, farther than they help to bring all pertaining to us into the obedience of Christ, is the way to hinder the work of God in our souls.

18. Acknowledge God in all the dispensations of his providence, as well as grace; for the evil as well as the good, is under his permission and control: and viewed in that light, are calculated to effect the best ends.

If we do not see God in all things, and all in God, we neither be, nor do, nor suffer right.

Extract

From a Sermon on SANCTIFICATION, *by the*
REV. JOSEPH SUTCLIFFE.

Having a few pages to spare, the editors take the liberty to subjoin the following observations from Mr. Sutcliffe's sermon, which, it is presumed, will perfectly accord with the sentiments so ably supported in the preceding essay.

After quoting a variety of sacred texts in proof of the doctrine of Christian perfection, the author proceeds to remark as follows:

"WITH REGARD TO THE way of obtaining sanctification in the higher sense of the word, faith and prayer are the means pointed out in the Scriptures. After the Lord, by Ezekiel, had enumerated the blessings of the new covenant, he adds, 'I will yet for this be inquired of by the house of Israel, to do it for them.' We must form a just and cautious estimate of the remains of sin in our hearts, which are ever ready to rekindle by the sparks of temptation; we must estimate the liberty to which we are called by the promises, and by the more advanced believers; for professors who look not for their privileges, are no models to those who are reaching forth to win the prize. We must close with the promises, and being greatly encouraged by what we daily receive, look for the Father and the Son, with the abiding Comforter, to make their abode with us; I would say, to cleanse, and to rule the heart.

"Another important point to be noticed is, that whatever degrees of holiness, and growing perfection of graces, young men in Christ may attain, there is yet a state of tried and suffered purity, which belongs exclusively to fathers. It is the state into which St. Peter prays that the scattered and persecuted Churches might enter. 'But the God of all grace, who hath called us unto his eternal glory by Christ Jesus, after that ye have suffered awhile, make you perfect, establish, strengthen, and settle you.' As a building established and settled on a rock is not to be moved by the tempest, so is the well tried Christian whose 'heart is established with grace.'

"In the selection of models of living holiness, to encourage our progress, considerable difficulties occur. Myriads of Christians, accounted regenerate because they have tasted that the Lord is gracious, have daily besetments of sinful propensities and tempers, which becloud their minds, and fetter their progress. But others have been so favoured as to retain their first love for a considerable time, and to walk in the light of the Lord, unconscious of any evil in their heart. Mecarius mentions a few whom he had known, who had enjoyed these comforts for five or six years; but afterwards evils were discovered to arise in their hearts.

"Consequently, the models of holiness are to be found only among the faithful Christians, who press towards the mark, and endure the conflicts of life in the years of their pilgrimage till they attain the promised land. And in all these exercises and trials of faith, God has the uniform design to wean our hearts from all inordinate attachments to the present world, and to place our whole desire on him alone.

"This good man; this pious and industrious man, for example, sees all the fruits of his labour, designed as the honey for the winter of life, taken away by false and imposing men, by conflagration, or by shipwreck. Nature feels the shock: the cloud of privations, for the moment, overshadows the soul. But recollection and confidence bring comfort. He softly says, 'I have yet a God, who has all resources in his hand. He is my exceeding great reward. I will cast myself on his mercy, and gratefully accept of an humbler path in life, which he, as my Father, points out for my course.'

"Another good man is surrounded by a rising and a hopeful family. 'The light of God is on his tabernacle; his children are about him; and the Lord pours him out butter from the rock.' But while in the visionary prospects of patriarchal felicity, his children are called away, some, perhaps, to fall in distant regions, while those at home droop and die. He sees his favourite son, now the hope of his house, or his most lovely daughter, come to the bloom of life and beauty, from whom he had contemplated the felicity of the nuptial day; oh! yes; he sees this most lovely child, as a flower bitten by the worm, droop, and languish, and die. This is the time of sacrifice, when the Christian is called to tread a suffering path, and sustain the bereavement of all his children. But here the good man rises in the strength of faith. He follows the souls of his children in the expectation of immortal hope. He sanctifies himself by the idea of meeting them in glory. His solicitude is, that he may be as holy and as happy as the children he has lost. He knows that God cannot err; and though unable to penetrate the depth of darker dispensations, yet while confiding in a God unseen, his soul becomes purified in the fire, and refined as the gold.

"Another good man, scarcely past the prime of life, and in the midst of his usefulness, and when a rising family are more and more dependant on his care, suddenly perceives his health to alter, and his strength to fail. He looks on his wife, and receives the return of her regards, neither of whom seem willing to discover all that they fear. He looks on his children who run about him unalarmed for the parent they must shortly lose. Often the tear starts in his eyes when he thinks of the ills of life to which they may be exposed. Often the secret prayer ascends to him who has said, 'I will be a husband to thy widow, and let thy fatherless children trust in me.' Nature, like the Saviour's humanity, deprecates the bitter cup; but religion, coming with all her aids, revives his soul with all the consolations of an immortal hope. He approaches more and more to the bosom of him who strikes, till he can say as the Saviour, 'Father, not as I will, but as thou wilt.' He firmly believes that God will hear and answer all his prayers for his family and for the church. Thus he acquires the perfection, the full ripe excellence of pure religion, and commends his spirit to God, 'in sure and certain hope of a resurrection to eternal life.'

"Brethren, I speak not here of the glory of our martyrs, and of the perfection, and faith, and piety, to which they attained when they went triumphant to the fire, or singing to the scaffold; or boldly, like the venerable Polycarp, took the lion by the mane. These are walks of faith and victory above the usual reach of men. Suffice to say, that there is a maturity of grace, or a degree of holiness, to be attained on earth, which raises a poor sinful worm, in some sort, to the language and sentiments of martyrs, and which cleanses the soul from all unrighteousness, and perfects it in love.

"We are called upon, in the next place, to defend the Scripture doctrine of Christian perfection, against the contumelious treatment it has received from high characters in the religious world. And surely there is no subject on which it is more to be regretted that good men should use language, and adopt systems, so much repugnant to each other. But the difference, after all, we would candidly hope, is greater in language than in sentiment. I translate for this purpose, some passages from Mr. John Calvin, whose Commentaries and Institutes are studied by great and respectable bodies of Christian ministers, and widely diffused through all the Protestant world.

"In his notes on Romans viith, and verse the 15th, he says, 'In this life, regeneration is only commenced; the remains of the flesh ever follow their corrupt affections, and make war against the mind.' At the 25th verse, he adds, 'The apostle confesses, that while grovelling here on earth, he ceased not to be loaded with much ordure or defilement.' 'I myself serve the law of sin.' Here is a most impressive passage to refute the cursed and unhappy doctrine of the Catharians, which certain weak headed people of our age are endeavouring to revive and enforce.'

"And on the 3d verse of the viiith chapter, 'The law of the Spirit of life which is in Christ Jesus, hath made me free from the law of sin and death,' he asks, 'Where is the man in all the world who has so far obtained angelic purity, as not to have the least remains of sin in his heart?' — Those who are in the flesh 'are destitute of all the grace of Christ, which belongs to none but the regenerate.'

On the 9th verse, he adds, 'It must not be admitted, that men walk after the Spirit because they are filled with the Spirit, which as yet is not the case with any one, but because they have the Spirit abiding with them; for they always feel some remains of sin dwelling in their hearts. Hence men are denominated carnal or spiritual according to the principle which predominates in their breasts.'

"On the 11th verse, 'He shall quicken your mortal bodies by his Spirit which dwelleth in you,' the same author assures us, 'That the apostle anticipates an objection, that how much soever the Spirit might possess one part of our nature, the other ever remained under the dominion of death. To which he replies, that the quickening power of the Spirit of God is able to swallow up and annihilate whatever is mortal in man. Consequently, we must patiently wait till the remains of sin be wholly abolished' [in the resurrection from the dead].

"When I consult this author on the great commandment, 'Thou shalt love the Lord thy God with all thy heart, and with all thy soul, and with all thy might,' I still find the same system uniformly supported. 'Though the saints,' he says, 'love God with their mind, and with sincere affection of heart; yet a very great part of their heart and soul is still occupied by the concupiscence of the flesh, by which they are obstructed and retarded in a speedy approach to God.'—To the doctrine delivered in these extracts, I would my brethren, take the following exceptions:

"1. That how correct soever this author's doctrine of indwelling sin may be, as to the great body of the Christian world, the standard of regeneration and religious attainments is below that of the New Testament; which represents the fathers in Christ as like their Saviour, and St. Stephen as praying for his enemies who were about to stone him. This martyr had not angelic perfection; but he had all the perfection of holiness which has ever been preached to the church, and held up as the mark after which we ought to aspire. It is surely the best and wisest to represent the standard of holiness as perfect, that we may ever be pressing after higher attainments.

"2. After making all due allowances for the barbarity of the age in which this author wrote, it seems injudicious and indelicate to represent St. Paul as never ceasing to be covered with the dung and filth of sin, while himself in twenty places speaks in very different language: 'that he was dead to sin; made free from sin; crucified to the world, and ready to be offered up.'

"3. It is quite unsupported to call the doctrine of the Catharians, (a sect of the primitive church, who preached purity,) *cursed and unhappy!* If these anathemas are levelled also against Kempis's Imitation of Jesus Christ, then the most popular book of the age, for one thing to be blamed in that work, it is a received opinion that a hundred are to be admired. And to deny that any one was ever filled with the Spirit, in opposition to very many texts of the New Testament, is certainly a very presumptive and extraordinary opinion. The Ephesians are exhorted 'not to be drunk with wine, wherein is excess, but to be filled with the Spirit.'"

"4. The pleas of this author for the predominant power of indwelling sin, in his comment on the 5th chapter of the epistle to the Galatians, that the flesh so lusted against the Spirit, that *they could not do* the things they would, fail to give the true sense of St. Paul, who declares that the churches of that province were fallen from grace by the controversy which Judaizing teachers had excited in favour of the Mosaic law. Hence we must not judge a good man by his moments of warmth, but rather imitate this apostle, who says, 'My little children, for whom I travail in birth until Christ be again formed in your heart, the hope of glory.' The true and proper use of this passage, is to warn the church, like the apostle, and apprize the strongest of believers, even those fathers who enjoy the abiding Comforter, and feel nothing in their hearts contrary to love, that if they watch not in the time of temptation, every evil may again spring up in their hearts, and with desolating force.

"5. The idea that the Spirit that dwelleth in us shall deliver us from the remains of sin by quickening our mortal bodies, now generally copied in our theological writings, is no other than a death purgatory, and a cheerless privation of all hope in the present world. We own that the doctrine has much apparent countenance from the present state of the body, which is mortal, sluggish, and even solicitous of indulgence. We own that no man can stand for a moment either justified or sanctified before his Maker without the merits of the Saviour. But why should sin be thus essentially identified with a body, which of itself can neither do good nor evil? Has not all sin its source in the heart? Are not all the functions of the body holy while the soul is led by the Spirit, and never sinful till they become inordinate and misdirected? All frail and defective as believers are, and liable to sin every moment, do not the Father, and the Son, and the Comforter, dwell in them as the temples of the Triune God? It is not judicious to affirm, that St. Paul, in his approaches to martyrdom, 'ceased not to be loaded with the ordure of sin,' and to represent, as our author repeatedly does, the whole unregenerate world as wholly destitute of grace, and their remorse of conscience as the mere judgment which the mind passes upon their actions, in order to say to the elect, that they are all perfect and complete in Christ. If sin have its seat in the soul, and there be no purgatory in a future state, why not allow the soul in its last act of faith, like St. Stephen, to be saved from the remains of pride, and malice, and unbelief, a few hours or moments before its exit from the body? Grant us but this one thing, and we ask no more; that we may the more 'give diligence unto the full assurance of hope unto the end;' Heb. vi, 11. — Grant us this one thing, which we boldly claim as our right, because the grave can save from nothing that is immoral. When the body of a saint, the hallowed temple of the Lord Most High, descends into the tomb, it is 'earth to earth, ashes to ashes, dust to dust.' It is not the man of sin, but the effects of sin, which become the prey of corruption. To save from the old man and the carnal enmity of the heart by perfect love, is not the office of the grave, but of the Sanctifier, who first formed man in his own image and who will finish his work, and cut it short in righteousness before and not after, the exit of the soul from the body."

Appendix
Biographical Sketch of Timothy Merritt

TIMOTHY MERRITT WAS BORN at Barkhamstead, Connecticut, October 12, 1775, to parents who were descended from stern Puritan ancestry. After he was converted in 1792, he joined the New England Conference, M. E. Church and entered the traveling connection in 1796. Rev. Merritt was stationed on the New London circuit, which at that time covered approximately 300 miles.

His next circuit was in the new Penobscot country, Maine, which was hardly opened out of the forest at that time. He "located" in 1803 in order to relieve the churches from the burden of supporting him and his growing family, and continued located for fourteen years. Nevertheless, he labored actively as a preacher while earning his own living during this entire time.

He returned to the traveling work in 1817, and filled important appointments until 1832. In that year he became assistant editor of *The Christian Advocate and Journal*, at New York, a position he held for four years. In 1831, while he was stationed at Malden, Massachusetts, he devoted a part of his time to the editorship of

Zion's Herald. He was appointed to the South Street church, Lynn, Massachusetts, in 1836, where he served for two years.

In 1838, Timothy Merritt took a superannuated relation. In 1839 he founded the magazine which became known as *The Guide to Holiness*, originally called *The Guide to Christian Perfection*.[73]

He died at Lynn, Massachusetts in 1845. He was a strong polemic writer in defense of the doctrines and polity of the church, and was a faithful preacher. During his lifetime he exerted a strong influence upon Sarah Lankford and her sister, Phoebe Palmer.

---

73. A detailed account of the magazine's history can be found in *Fragrant Memories*, by George Hughes, published by Schmul Publishing Co.

Bibliographic Resources for Holiness Literature

Dayton, Donald W. *The American Holiness Movement: A Bibliographic Introduction*. The First in a Series of "Occasional Bibliographical Papers of the B. L. Fisher Library. Wilmore, KY: B. L. Fisher Library, Asbury Theological Seminary, 1971. This is a groundbreaking work that provides an important overview and contextualization of Holiness literature.

Jones, Charles Edwin. *Black Holiness: A Guide to the Study of Black Participation in Wesleyan Perfectionist and Glossolalic Pentecostal Movements*. Metuchen, NJ and London: The American Theological Library Association and The Scarecrow Press, 1987. While this resource includes extensive information on Pentecostal developments, it also provides helpful data on Black Holiness denominations and such leaders as Charles Price Jones, founder of the Church of Christ (Holiness) U.S.A., and Black participation in primarily white Holiness denominations, such as Jerry Miles Humphrey, evangelist in the Free Methodist Church.

———. *A Guide to the Study of the Holiness Movement*. Metuchen, NJ: The Scarecrow Press and The American Theological Library Association, 1974. While superseded in some ways by Jones's

The Wesleyan Holiness Movement: A Comprehensive Guide, this earlier groundbreaking work remains valuable in its own right.

―――. *The Wesleyan Holiness Movement: A Comprehensive Guide.* ATLA Bibliography Series, no. 50 Vol. One and Vol. Two. Lanham, MD: The Scarecrow Press and The American Theological Library Association, 2005. This catalogs many important reprints as well as original publications and is an invaluable guide to the subject.

Kostlevy, William, Gari-Anne Patzwald, and Wallace Thornton, Jr., eds. *Historical Dictionary of the Holiness Movement*, Third edition. Lanham, MD: Rowman and Littlefield, 2024. Each edition of this work provides a helpful bibliography in addition to numerous brief biographical entries for Holiness authors.

―――.. *Holiness Manuscripts: A Guide to Sources Documenting the Wesleyan Holiness Movement in the United States and Canada.* Metuchen, NJ and London: The American Theological Library Association and The Scarecrow Press, 1994. In addition to correspondence and other manuscripts, this work provides helpful information regarding Holiness periodicals.

Long, Gene. *A Survey of Holiness Literature* Vol. 1: Early Church Fathers to 1900. Salem, OH: Allegheny Publications, 2005, and *A Survey of Holiness Literature* Vol. 2: 1901 to Today. Salem, OH: Allegheny Publications, 2010. While helpful, this work should be evaluated in consultation with other resources, as it does contain some significant errors, such as suggesting that Ralph Earle (well known Church of the Nazarene biblical scholar and translator) was the son of A. B. Earle, an early Holiness advocate among the Baptists, which was not the case.

Miller, William Charles, ed. *Holiness Works: A Bibliography: A Revised Edition of The Master Bibliography of Holiness Works* (Kansas City, MO: Nazarene Theological Seminary, Nazarene Publishing

House, 1986). While produced under the auspices of Nazarene Theological Seminary, this guide helpfully highlights prominent devotional, theological, and biographical works from various traditions related to the Holiness Movement.

Vincent, John Paul. *One Professor's Lifetime of Reflection and Reading on Holiness*. Ed. by Mark R. Elliot. Wilmore, KY: First Fruits Press, 2022. This work presents personal reactions and insights in a biographical account of interactions with Holiness literature along with "An Annotated Bibliography of Selected Holiness Literature."

Wilcox, Leslie. *Be Ye Holy: A Study of the Teaching of Scripture Relative to Entire Sanctification with A Sketch of the History and the Literature of the Holiness Movement* Revised Edition (Salem, OH: Schmul Publishing Co., 1994). This proves to be one of the most helpful guides to Holiness literature, providing succinct evaluations of various works in historical or biographical contexts.

MEMBERS OF SCHMUL'S WESLEYAN BOOK
CLUB BUY THESE OUTSTANDING BOOKS AT
40% OFF THE RETAIL PRICE

Join Schmul's Wesleyan Book Club by calling toll-free:
$$800\text{-}S_7P_7B_2O_6O_6K_5S_7$$
Put a discount Christian bookstore in your
own mailbox

Visit us on the Internet at
www.wesleyanbooks.com

Schmul Publishing Company | PO Box 776 | Nicholasville, KY 40340

www.ingramcontent.com/pod-product-compliance
Lightning Source LLC
Chambersburg PA
CBHW070151100426
42743CB00013B/2879